A Tennessee Christmas

Written and Compiled by
JAN KIEFER

Foreword by
JOSEPH E. JOHNSON

Photography by
DAVID CROSBY

WESTCLIFFE PUBLISHERS

ENGLEWOOD, COLORADO

WE WOULD LIKE TO EXPRESS SPECIAL THANKS TO:
John Rice Irwin and Phila Hach, who so generously introduced us to their Tennessee; Amy Kottmeyer, who so capably ran the Tennessee Taste Test; Kim Tuton, who kindly helped with the keystroking; Tourism Commissioner John Wade; and, most especially, our families—Joy, Laurel, and John David Crosby, and Melissa Kiefer—who encouraged us and shared many of the challenges and opportunities of this project.

—J.K. and D.C.

INTERNATIONAL STANDARD BOOK NUMBER
1-56579-295-5

EDITOR: Suzanne Venino
DESIGNER: Rebecca Finkel, F + P Graphic Design
PRODUCTION MANAGER: Harlene Finn

TEXT
© 1998 Jan Kiefer. ALL RIGHTS RESERVED.

PHOTOGRAPHY
© 1998 David Crosby. ALL RIGHTS RESERVED.

LIBRARY OF CONGRESS CATALOGING-IN-PUBLICATION DATA
Kiefer, Jan.
  A Tennessee Christmas / text by Jan
Kiefer ; photography by David Crosby ;
foreword by Joseph E. Johnson.
    p. cm.
  ISBN 1-56579-295-5
  1. Christmas—Tennessee.
  2. Christmas cookery—Tennessee.
  3. Tennessee—Social life and customs.
  I. Title.
GT4896.T2K54 1998   98-18889
394.2663'09768—dc21   CIP

PUBLISHER
Westcliffe Publishers, Inc.
P.O. Box 1261
Englewood, Colorado 80150

PRINTED IN HONG KONG
THROUGH WORLD PRINT LTD

All items in this book were either submitted as original material or are reprinted with permission. Neither Westcliffe Publishers nor Jan Kiefer is responsible for any misrepresentation of origin.

For information about other fine books and calendars from Westcliffe Publishers, please call your local bookstore, contact us at 1-800-523-3692, or write for our free color catalog.

FIRST FRONTISPIECE: Fall Creek Falls
SECOND FRONTISPIECE: Citrus fruit studded with cloves, surrounded by natural Christmas greens and berries

TABLE OF CONTENTS

Snowy gate, New Year's morning, Rugby

QUICK REFERENCE

FOREWORD

Christmas at our house means one thing above all: family. The four of us humans, plus our four-legged companions, enjoy a day of splendid isolation, scented with evergreens and succulent roasting meats.

Ever since Pat and I married, it has been our tradition to celebrate Christmas in our own home. Our parents were a little miffed when we announced this decision, but thankfully the rifts quickly healed. And our children, Kent and Kelly, always slept well on Christmas Eve, knowing that Santa knew exactly where to find them. Long before Christmas Day, we begin to make ready. I expect that our preparations are recreated by thousands of Tennesseeans from Memphis to Mountain City during the Yuletide season.

The holiday begins officially when we decorate the tree— a real tree. One that we can smell. Our ornament collection can most kindly be described as eclectic. There are lopsided, glittery things the children made when they were small, a few ornaments reminiscent of our beloved University of Tennessee, a tattered partridge in a pear tree that started married life with us, and, atop the tree, a black Labrador retriever dressed as an angel, in honor of our dog Duchess.

Pat begins shopping for presents months before Christmas. I must confess that I'm a Christmas Eve shopper. I don't put it off; I just spend a great deal of time planning. We buy lots of gifts. Not for us the single, pricey item such as a leather armchair or passage to Bora Bora. Our gifts aren't extravagant, but they're plentiful. We always have a fire in the fireplace on Christmas Day, even though with Tennessee's unpredictable weather, we sometimes have to open the windows to moderate the indoor temperature.

Falls Mill, Franklin County

When we gather to open gifts, we settle in for awhile. Each person in turn takes center stage to unwrap a present—a round robin we repeat until the floor is piled high with ribbon and boxes and each of us has said "thank you" 117 times. Duchess and Casper the cat get gifts, too, as well as tidbits of the standing rib roast that is our holiday meal of choice.

Simple traditions, lovingly nurtured over a lifetime. That is our Christmas, a Tennessee Christmas that I would not exchange for the most elaborate in the world. I invite you to sit back and enjoy *A Tennessee Christmas,* a celebration of traditions, events, and sights that will certainly put you in the holiday spirit. Merry Christmas!

Dr. Joseph E. Johnson is the nineteenth president of the University of Tennessee.
From his office in Knoxville he oversees the operation of the entire university
system, which includes four primary campuses and three statewide institutes.

PREFACE

My Scottish grandfather was a staunch Presbyterian, having come over from the old country as a youngster. He believed in God, family, education, and the land, and we were never in doubt about his convictions. My early memories include having to memorize scripture verses before we could open our Christmas gifts. My brothers and I both loved and feared this larger-than-life figure who fed us endless tidbits of interesting information as well as lengthy sermons on his favorite subjects. His ample pockets always kept us well supplied with balloons.

In his desire to see that his own three children, including my mother, were properly educated in a Godly manner, he researched Presbyterian colleges and ended up sending all three to Maryville College in Tennessee. As long as I can remember, my family has sung the praises of beautiful Tennessee and of the many happy experiences they had there.

Years later, when my parents were overseas medical missionaries, my brother and I attended boarding school in North Carolina. After spending a Christmas in Indianapolis with relatives, we were on a bus traveling back to school. Almost the minute we crossed into Tennessee, snow started falling, draping the countryside in Christmas splendor and obliterating all traces of winter brown. That day I experienced not only the beauty of Tennessee, but also the kindness of its people.

Somewhere between the Kentucky line and Knoxville, the bus slowed to a crawl due to treacherous roads, but by that time I no longer noticed because I was suffering from a severe bout of malaria (a residual illness from a childhood spent in Africa). As the bus pulled into Knoxville, I was wracked with pain, nausea, and fever. I have no specific memory of the bus station or the fellow passengers who helped me, but I do remember their gentleness and kindness as they cared for a child, a stranger in their midst that Christmas season.

Having lived a number of years across the border in both North Carolina and Georgia, I have often made Tennessee a destination for weekend outings, vacations, and holidays. Many of my own Christmas memories include Chattanooga and Dayton. I have established many friendships in Tennessee and it is a place I return to often.

Researching this book has given me an even greater appreciation of the strength of spirit and the generosity of the people of Tennessee. From every corner of the state, photographer David Crosby and I were welcomed with open hearts. We have truly enjoyed our time spent chronicling Tennessee holiday traditions and visiting the many beautiful places that are the heart and soul of this great state.

To everyone who reads this book, our wish is that you too enjoy how wonderful it is to be a part of a Tennessee Christmas.

Jan E. Kiefer

Little red cabin, Pleasant Valley

Dedicated with love to my mother, Charlotte King Kraay,

who spent some of her happiest years in Tennessee, and

who has been my greatest support in this effort.

—J.K.

A Tennessee Perspective

The pages of Tennessee history are peppered with illustrious names, such as Presidents Andrew Jackson, James Polk, and Andrew Johnson; and, of course, their wives: Rachel Jackson, Sarah Polk, and Eliza Johnson. Noted military men hailed from Tennessee: Sam Davis, Nathan Bedford Forrest, John Hunt Morgan, and World War I hero Sergeant York. Father of the United Nations and Nobel Peace Prize winner Cordell Hull came from Tennessee. Governor John Sevier—often referred to as the "Father of Tennessee"—was also the governor of Franklin, which lost its bid to become a state by only one vote. Nancy Ward, a powerful Cherokee, took part in the War Councils, and at least once she saved the life of a white man about to be burned at the stake. Sam Houston once owned a farm and taught school in rural Blount County. Author James Agee, born and raised in Tennessee, set his book *A Death in the Family* here, as did Alex Haley with his Pulitzer Prize–winning epic novel *Roots*. And who could forget legendary railroadman Casey Jones?

The list of famous Tennesseans could go on for many pages, but it was the countless un-named individuals who forged this land into the great state it is today. Early pioneers faced the formidable Appalachian Mountains as they pressed westward in search of a place to settle and call home. They also experienced many fierce encounters with Indians loathe to relinquish their ancestral lands, and a great price was paid for the settlement of many parcels of land.

During the early 1800s, the settlers had made considerable progress, both in the mountains of East Tennessee and in West Tennessee, where a thriving Mississippi River economy was developing in Memphis. Near Nashville and throughout Middle Tennessee, vast plantations provided crops of cotton and other staples, which were then transported via the Mississippi River to other parts of the country. A vibrant agricultural economy and trade had developed throughout the state. On its way to Atlanta, the great north/south railroad ran through rapidly growing Chattanooga.

Top: Musket loading, Manskers Station re-enactment, Goodlettsville
Bottom: Mantle decorated for the holidays, Manskers Station re-enactment

Left: Tennessee fireplace, Franklin
Overleaf: Rolling farmland near Jonesborough

Perhaps the greatest challenge the people of Tennessee had to face was the Civil War. Because Tennessee was part of the South, yet was located north of Atlanta, it stood in the way of advancing Union armies. Not only was the state ravaged by both Union and Confederate soldiers, but thousands of Tennessee lives were also lost. A great human toll was exacted at major battle sites such as Missionary Ridge and Shiloh. Today, the Civil War dead are remembered throughout Tennessee with monuments and parks.

With an indomitable frontier spirit, the people of Tennessee kept the faith. Supported by the strength of their legendary close-knit families, they quickly put the war behind them and set about to rebuild their land. These days Tennessee is known for more peaceful pursuits. It is the center of some of the country's greatest music and home to some of the nation's most beautiful tourist attractions. Behind it all, from the small towns and bustling cities, are the people themselves. As they gather with their families at Christmas, the people of Tennessee can be proud to be part of the history that has made this state great.

Christopher Taylor House, Jonesborough

Redcoats muster at Fort Louden Christmas re-enactment

The Hunt-Phelan Home

The festive aromas of pine, cinnamon, and cloves hang in the air, and holiday visitors to the Hunt-Phelan Home are in for a special treat—an old-fashioned Christmas candlelight tour of one of the most beautiful and historic homes on legendary Beale Street in Memphis. Replicating holiday decorations of the late nineteenth century, the mansion is tastefully decorated with greens and other natural items. Docents dressed in authentic period costumes make the past come alive as they guide groups through the house, relating the history of the residence and its remarkable owners, the Hunt-Phelans, a wealthy and politically influential family.

During the 1800s, when this river town was growing into a thriving city, Beale Street was home to Memphis' wealthiest and most renowned families. Designed by famed architect Robert Mills (well known for designing many famous buildings, such as the United States Treasury in Washington, DC and the Fireproof Building in Charleston, South Carolina), the Hunt-Phelan Home was constructed between the years 1828 and 1832. The house was a center of social and political activity, and frequent visitors included Jefferson Davis, Nathan Bedford Forrest, and Andrew Jackson. During the Civil War, General Ulysses S. Grant commandeered the property as Union Headquarters. The plans for the Battle of Vicksburg were formulated in the library, which Grant used as his office. Following Grant's departure, the house was used as a hospital for Union soldiers. After the war, one of the country's first Freedman Bureau Schools was founded on the grounds, providing education to the children of former slaves.

Today, the Hunt-Phelan Home has been meticulously restored, with exquisite antique china, silver, and furnishings, some dating back as far as the seventeenth century. The mansion also houses an astounding collection of Civil War era photographs, journals, maps, and books, including rare first editions. The collection documents much of Memphis' history during the war. The Hunt-Phelan Home's significance to the history of Memphis, Tennessee, and to the United States is evident to visitors who tour this gracious nineteenth-century home.

Above: Hunt-Phelan Home formal dining room

Left: Victorian Christmas tree and antique dolls at the Hunt-Phelan Home, oldest house in Memphis

Historic Rugby

Nestled in the mountains of East Tennessee, the English colony of Rugby celebrated its first American Christmas in 1880. The colonists spent time visiting with each other, hunting, singing, feasting, and, most of all, remembering their friends and families back in England.

Christ Church Episcopal held Christmas services, and the sanctuary was "prettily decorated," as reported by the local paper, *The Rugbeian:* "The walls were decorated with mottoes made of white letters in wool, faced with evergreens on red ground. On the west wall the word 'Emmanuel' was surmounted by a star and surrounded by various emblematic devices, connected by wreaths of evergreen. A similar device appeared on the east wall, while the pulpit and reading desk were tastefully adorned with initials in wool, embedded in leaves."

The town's busy commissary carried such items as imported toys, candies, baby bottles, rattles, cards, books, musical instruments, colognes, and "hair restorers for the old, hair beautifiers for the young." It also stocked the ingredients to make traditional English Christmas pudding. The word "welcome" fashioned from holly and hemlock greeted the shoppers.

Founded by author Thomas Hughes in 1880, the town of Rugby grew rapidly. Today, seventeen of the original buildings still stand, including the Hughes Public Library, which contains more than 7,000 volumes and is essentially unchanged since it was built in 1882. It is to these historic buildings that holiday visitors come each year to recapture the feeling of Old England during self-guided candlelight and lantern-lit tours.

For two nights in December, hosts in period costumes graciously welcome visitors as they arrive in town, which has been lavishly decorated with greenery. Visitors attend services at Christ Church, shop at the commissary, and sip hot wassail fireside at the Rugby Community Room. They can join in singing with carolers strolling through the village, where the lovely sounds of flutes and psaltery fill the wintry air. Upon leaving, visitors take with them an insight into the life of colonists who settled small Tennessee towns like Rugby.

I remember Granddaddy Wise would arrive with loads of oranges and apples that tasted wonderful.

—LINDA WISE-TUCKER,
formerly of Miner Hill

Hughes Public Library,
Historic Rugby

THE FIRST CHRISTMAS IN RUGBY

As reported in *The Rugbeian*, January 1881, and now read aloud each Christmas during holiday celebrations.

For several days before Christmas Day, foreshadowing of the festive occasion was heralded by the arrival of seasonable cards sent by loving hearts in old England, to spirited sons and daughters who have for the first time absented themselves from that loving company to take up their abode in this enchanting spot of the new world.

Christmas pudding fever found its way to each house hold, and our American residents, although impervious to such ravages in the past, fell victim to the current malady. Anglo-American exertions were put forth at the Tabard and in private dwellings, to decorate walls in true English style.

Nature was bountiful in a rich supply of red-berried, rich green-leafed holly; but alas! the mistletoe was hunted for by both sexes in vain. It was suggested that a few dozen roots of this be imported from England. Young ladies and matrons vied with each other in the best production and decoration of plum pudding; they were each, however, compelled to labor in the sad disadvantage of having no suet nor candied lemon, such necessary ingredients not having arrived in the colony.

The day was heralded by sharp frost and snow; the innumerable lovely pine trees were covered with a mantle of purity. Young gentlemen and sturdy artisans went shooting deer and wild turkeys, which thanks to a beneficent providence, are plentiful here. The young ladies made morning calls of salutation. Each of the wanderers returned to their respective homes punctually, and with such heartiness that it would have gladdened the eye of English friends at home to have witnessed. Ample justice having been done to the bountifully supplied tables, and the accustomed silent wish in partaking of the first mince pie having been duly performed, a toast to Old England, Her Homes and Firesides, was given....

As we wish to be practical in any notice we may take of proceedings in the colony, we hope that this mode of keeping Christmas festivities will, like leaven, permeate throughout the states. Our only regret is that owing to the church building's not being completed, religious service of praise and thanksgiving could not be held. We were, however, cheered to hear the lovely sweet voices of many of our colonists singing the ever accepted hymn: "Hark the Herald Angels Sing."

Snowy street in Rugby

Christmas in our family was frugal. Each of the children received only one nice toy, like a doll, toy stove, or a set of lead "Tootsietoys," and one item of necessary clothing, such as pajamas, a robe, or slippers. Our stockings were filled with an orange, an apple, and nuts.

—NANCY WAGGENER KING,
formerly of Nashville

Tennessee Plantation Christmas

The "Antebellum Homes Capital of Tennessee" is what the towns of Columbia, Mount Pleasant, and Spring Hill call themselves. Each year in December these towns present an annual two-day Christmas "pilgrimage" of eleven area plantations and other historic buildings. From Revolutionary War land-grant homes to those of Civil War note, each house is decorated for the holidays, with self-guided tours of the interiors and the grounds. Many of the mansions are privately owned, making this Christmas viewing particularly special.

RATTLE & SNAP PLANTATION, Mount Pleasant

Unrivaled in beauty, this 1845 Greek revival mansion holds the distinction of being one of the finest restored plantations in the nation. Colonel William Polk won the tract of land, an acquired Revolutionary War land grant, from the governor of North Carolina, who had wagered 5,648 acres in a game of dice. Colonel Polk commemorated his good fortune by naming his new property Rattle & Snap after the game of chance.

Entering through wrought-iron gates, guests pass by a period re-enactment, with a small detachment of soldiers in Civil War uniforms. The soldiers are more than willing to put down their muskets and escort ladies up to the gleaming white columns of the mansion. Inside the house, visitors are treated to a spectacular fifteen-foot Christmas tree standing in the foyer. The home is furnished with antiques of the period, one of the most beautiful of which is the candolier in the dining room. Guests with prior reservations for the holiday luncheon at the Rattle & Snap have the pleasure of feasting on turkey cooked in the plantation's kitchen.

Above: Confederate soldiers stage a re-enactment outside Rattle & Snap Plantation

Right: Sixteen-foot Christmas tree in foyer of Rattle & Snap

BEECHLAWN, Columbia

A beautifully preserved Greek revival home built circa 1860, Beechlawn briefly served as the headquarters for Civil War Generals John Schofield, John Bell Hood, and Nathan Bedford Forrest during the winter of 1864. Filled with family antiques and treasures, Beechlawn was once the home of Amos and Cornelia Warfield, who lived in a log cabin on the property during the seven years it took to complete the house. This historic cabin, along with an old ice house, are also available for viewing.

WALNUT GROVE, Mount Pleasant

In 1863, Union troops raided the cotton crop at Walnut Grove. Outraged at the robbery, owner Sabra Lawrence, a seventy-six-year-old widow, followed the soldiers to Columbia where she demanded— and was given—$4,000 by the Union general. One of the features of Walnut Grove is the detached brick kitchen, which was typical of plantations of the time, so as not to heat up the rest of the house while cooking. Present owners have filled the home with a collection of English antiques and many original family pieces.

PRESIDENT JAMES K. POLK HOME, Columbia

The ancestral home of James K. Polk, the nation's eleventh president, this house contains many of the furnishings that were used by President Polk and his wife, Sarah, during his term. Aside from the White House, this charming home in downtown Columbia is the only house that Polk lived in that still exists. It has recently been restored, and during the Christmas season it takes on a special ambience with authentic holiday decorations.

Top: Beechlawn Plantation
Bottom: Warfield Cabin
at Beechlawn

RIPPAVILLA PLANTATION, Spring Hill

This stately twenty-two-room home was built in the mid-1850s for Major Nathaniel Cheair. Recently restored, it now serves as a Civil War Armies museum and a regional visitors' center. Because it was directly situated on the route taken by both Confederate and Union soldiers as they marched through Tennessee, the plantation's history is heavily entwined with the Civil War.

Rippavilla Plantation

 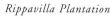

CEDARWINDS, Columbia

Site of considerable action during the war, the grounds of Cedarwinds served as an encampment for Confederate soldiers. Today Cedarwinds remains as stately and beautiful as when it was built in 1851. Most of the lumber used to build the home was cut on the property; bricks for the foundation and great fireplace were also made on site.

MULBERRY HILL, Columbia

A mansion with a colorful past, Mulberry Hill was built in the late 1820s on what was once part of General Nathanael Greene's 25,000-acre Revolutionary War land grant. One of its previous occupants was Confederate hero "Dunc" Cooper, a nineteen-year-old colonel who was held in great esteem for his many deeds of bravery while leading a band of guerrilla fighters against the Union Army.

SAM WATKINS-HARRIS-WEBSTER HOME, Columbia

Well-known Civil War writer Sam Watkins lived in this home before joining the Confederate Army. Civil War buffs know Watkins for his book *Co. Aytch,* which is considered one of the best personal memoirs of the war, as it is told from the viewpoint of a common soldier, or "high private," as Sam considered himself.

WILLIAM JAMES FRIERSON HOME, Columbia

When early settlers arrived in Columbia in 1807 to establish Zion Presbyterian Church, they first built a log church, then their own log homes. It was not until the following year that William James Frierson, the first clerk of the session at Zion, built his cabin, which now serves as the kitchen. The Frierson family lived here for more than 140 years. Today it is owned by a direct descendant of writer Sam Watkins.

ZION PRESBYTERIAN CHURCH, Columbia

Members of Zion Presbyterian Church built this structure in 1849 on General Nathanael Greene's Revolutionary War land grant. Time and materials were supplied on the basis of a member's ability to give. The front lawn of the church is a cemetery, with graves dating from the Revolutionary War, the War of 1812, and the Civil War.

THE ATHENAEUM

A strange but stunning combination of Moorish design and Gothic revival style, the Athenaeum was built in 1835 by President James K. Polk's nephew, Samuel Polk Walker. It later served as the rectory for Columbia Athenaeum, a prestigious girls' school that stood nearby.

The Hermitage

Stately and grand, the Hermitage was once the home of President Andrew Jackson. Construction on the mansion was first started in 1819. After it was burned in a fire in 1834, the mansion was rebuilt, and it was to this newly refurbished Hermitage that Jackson returned when he left the White House 1837.

The widowed Jackson (his wife, Rachel, had died before he was elected president) lived here with his adopted son, his daughter-in-law, her sister, and six children—

five of them boys. While there is little documented information on how Christmases were spent at the Hermitage, it is likely, based on historical accounts of the time, that the boys reveled in shooting off firecrackers and guns to celebrate the holiday. While president, Jackson hosted an annual New Year's reception at the White House, inviting politicians and diplomats to the lavish affair. He enjoyed giving parties, and he most likely also entertained at the Hermitage during the holiday season.

The Hermitage, near Nashville

Today at Christmas, the Hermitage, which is listed on the National Register of Historic Places, is decorated as it might have been in Jackson's day—sparingly with greenery, using whatever foliage was available, and perhaps adding flowers. It is unlikely that there were Christmas trees at that time. Modern Christmas celebrations at the Hermitage include performances by local music groups, evening tours, and children's craft classes. Perhaps the most charming holiday activity is the annual children's tea party, where youngsters dress up and experience afternoon tea as was held in the mid-nineteenth century.

The Holly and the Ivy

Moderately fast, but smoothly.

The Hol - ly and the I - vy Now both are full well grown; -- Of all the trees that spring in wood The Hol - ly bears the crown; -- The Hol - ly bears a blos - som As white as li - ly flower, And Ma - ry bore sweet Je - sus Christ, To be our sweet Sa - voir, -- To be our sweet Sa - vior ---

The Holly bears a berry
　　As red as any blood;
And Mary bore sweet Jesus Christ
　　To do poor sinners good.
The Holly bears a prickle
　　As sharp as any thorn;
And Mary bore Sweet Jesus Christ
　　On Christmas day in the morn.
On Christmas day in the morn.

The Holly bears a bark
　　As bitter as any gall;
And Mary bore sweet Jesus Christ
　　For to redeem us all.
The Holly and the Ivy
　　Now both are full well grown;
Of all the trees that spring in wood
　　The Holly bears the crown,
The Holly bears the crown.

Big South Fork of the Cumberland River

The Eugene Oliver place,
Cades Cove

Alex Stewart
A TENNESSEE PIONEER

Alex Stewart, the second of sixteen children, was born in 1891 in Newman's Ridge, Tennessee, in a tiny one-room cabin. For ninety-four years he lived what he considered a good life, most of it in a small cabin at Panther Creek, not far from Sneedville. He was a husband, father, grandfather, great-grandfather, and great-great-grandfather. But he was also a homesteader, a farmer, a craftsman (cooper, carver, and carpenter), and mountain philosopher. Stewart's life in Tennessee has been colorfully chronicled by John Rice Irwin, an authority on the Appalachian way of life and founder of the Museum of Appalachia in Norris, Tennessee. Mr. Irwin met and interviewed Alex Stewart in 1962, collecting an oral history of life in the mountains of Appalachia. The following are Alex Stewart's responses. They reflect the simplicity, dignity, and grace typical of rural Tennessee at the turn of the century.

THE FIRST CHRISTMAS TREE EVER I KNOWED of was put up by the Presbyterians who had come in here and built a churchhouse down on Blackwater. I's about ten years old, and nobody had never seen such before. The people just went crazy about it. Miss Axel (one of the Presbyterian missionaries) got me to make her a lot of toys to put on the tree; little pistols and things like that. And, oh, the stuff she put on the tree for me, for doing that: a knife, a French harp—that like'd to have tickled me to death.

THE FIRST PRESENT I EVER REMEMBER Pap getting us for Christmas was a little candy and an orange. I'll never forget that. I wasn't over four or five years old. I saved that candy and just took a little bite off it every once in a while. I don't know how long it lasted me. And they didn't have no decorations along back then. That come in later on.

Having heard references to "Old Christmas," but unable to obtain any first-hand information, John Rice Irwin asked Alex Stewart if he had ever heard of it.

OLD CHRISTMAS

Oh, yeah, they call it Piffiny [Epiphany] now. Today, lots of people don't believe in Old Christmas, by the way they talk. If you don't believe what I'm fixing to tell you, why you try it and you'll find out whether it's right or not.

On Old Christmas night at twelve o'clock, you go to where there's any cattle, and you go and sit down and listen to them pray. I tried that twice. The first time, it liked to have scared me to death. They got to going on so, that I broke and run back to the house. But I got to studying about it and then I tried it again. Me and my oldest sister went together, on one Old Christmas night. We went to the barn and set down and waited till about twelve o'clock, and just slipped up right easy, didn't make no racket. We had two milk cows, and directly they commenced. Just moo-o-o-o-o, moo-o-o-o-o-, and groaning and getting on, and we got scared and run to the house. Grandpap Stewart told me they'd do that, but I didn't believe it.

Decorated barn, near Johnson City

And after I'd tried it twice, I saw they was something to it. And I don't care how cold it is, nor how deep the ground is froze, elder bushes will sprout out of the ground on Old Christmas night. They'll sprout out that night and never get no bigger till the sap rises in the spring of the year. If you don't believe me, you find you a place where there's a bunch of elders a-growin' and you look around underneath the bushes the night before Old Christmas, and you won't see any sprouts. Then you go back the next morning and you'll see them sprouts a peeping through the ground everywhere, don't matter how hard the ground is froze. I've checked that out, I don't know at the times. And don't ever loan anything to anybody, if you can help it, on Old Christmas, because you're not apt to get it back.

—Excerpted from ALEX STEWART: PORTRAIT OF A PIONEER by John Rice Irwin.
Reprinted with permission.

CHRISTMAS AS IT USED TO BE
by Dick Poplin, Shelbyville

In the far off 20s and 30s, Christmas wasn't a one-day holiday. Christmas lasted all the way through to New Year's Day. Actually, it began on the Monday after Thanksgiving, when we scraped the pilgrims and turkeys off the schoolroom windows and pasted up Santa Clauses, Christmas trees and bells, and began to rehearse for the Christmas program. We had the holiday feeling for four weeks while we sang Jingle Bells, O' Little Town of Bethlehem, Silent Night and all the rest, and while we practiced the parts of shepherds, wise men and angels.

School let out on the Friday before Christmas. We had no classes that day and had our Christmas program in the afternoon. Names had been drawn and gifts bought—"nothing over a quarter, children"—and the cedar tree, which some of the older students had been privileged to help bring in from the nearby woods, was standing on the stage. The morning was occupied with putting the star and the tinsel on the tree and the packages on and under it. The schoolroom had the pleasant smell of cedar and oranges. Some of my wealthier schoolmates who had oranges before Christmas brought them on this last day of school and generously passed them around. I've often wondered why orange peelings tasted so good then but don't now.

There was something of a letdown after school closing, as there were still several days until Christmas. Some of those days were spent helping cut wood for the parlor fireplace. Other days were passed just fooling around, savoring the spicy aromas from the kitchen and shooting firecrackers. In those days every country store had a good supply of sparklers, Roman candles, sky rockets, spit devils, torpedoes and all sizes of firecrackers up to the five-inch ones that sold three for a dime.

Our Christmas gifts consisted mostly of candy and fruit that the kind Old Gentleman left in the shoe boxes set out for him. None of that hanging up stockings for us. The first thing I would get from my box would be an orange. I would cut a hole in the top of it, push a half stick of peppermint candy down into it and suck out the juice through the candy.

Christmas Day was usually family day. Either we were at home with near relatives or we went to an aunt's in town twenty miles away. At her house, the place would be swarming with relatives, some of whom we saw only at Christmas. On following days we visited other kin and neighbors or they visited us. We had Christmas dinners from December 25 to January 1, three or four at our house and three or four away. We didn't speak of Christmas Day. It was Christmas Week.

During the week there would be popcorn balls to munch between meals or before bedtime. Sometimes we made molasses candy, which required a candy pulling. Pleasant time was spent during these days just doing nothing and going nowhere or wandering through fields and woods where we found crossvine and rabbit tobacco, which our parents—although very opposed to smoking real tobacco—allowed us to smoke openly.

For several obvious reasons a Christmas such as we had then cannot be now. There isn't time. That much food would cost a fortune. Those calories would overwhelm us. But as long as I live, I can tell my children and grandchildren, "We just don't have Christmases like we used to anymore."

—*Reprinted with permission from* A YARD OF POPLIN *by Dick Poplin, published by Bell Buckle Press, 1991.*

When I was a boy many years ago, the highlight of Christmas was having firecrackers to shoot and an orange in the toe of my stocking.

—JOE PHILLIPS,
Johnson City

Horse-drawn sled, Museum of Appalachia, Norris

CHRISTMAS CARD SNOW
by Richard M. "Pek" Gunn
(1903 to 1995) Tennessee Poet Laureate

We had a snow sometime ago
  That brought us lots of cheer,
For Christmas Eve at last had come
  And Santa Claus was near.

The snow came down with such a hush
  And built throughout the night
Scintillating fairy land
  That filled us with delight.

The trees were heavily bedecked
  With globules crystal-clear
Like countless sparkling prisms hung
  On nature's chandelier.

And from our window we could see
  Old winter having fun
A trillion flakes like diamond chips
  Were glistening in the sun.

The redbirds and the chickadees
  All darting here and there
Gave color to the whiteness
  Of the snowflakes in the air.

Our place was like a wonderland
  For all about the yard
Were lovely scenes like artists paint
  Upon a Christmas Card.

Reprinted with permission from
GLOBAL FEASTING, TENNESSEE STYLE
by Phila Hach

Christmas was a warm, wonderful time for us.
Snow has a way of making even a humble shack
look magical and inviting. Christmas will always
be certain images to me: the glow of the fire through
the windows, the crackle of a pine knot burning,
even the smoke that seemed to reach out and pull
you by the nose into the house.

—FROM DOLLY BY DOLLY PARTON
Copyright 1994, Dolly Parton. Used by
arrangement with Harper Collins Publishers, Inc.

My home was in Nashville on a steep hill that was great for speedy
sledding in Christmas snow, but it ended dangerously on a busy
boulevard. I was brave enough to try it only once, and then with
someone else steering, so we would be sure to end up on a side
bank at the bottom.
—NANCY WAGGENER KING,
formerly of Nashville

Fraser firs along the Appalachian Trail

Still, Still, Still

Austrian Carol
Arranged by Frank Oros
Lyrics by Frank Oros

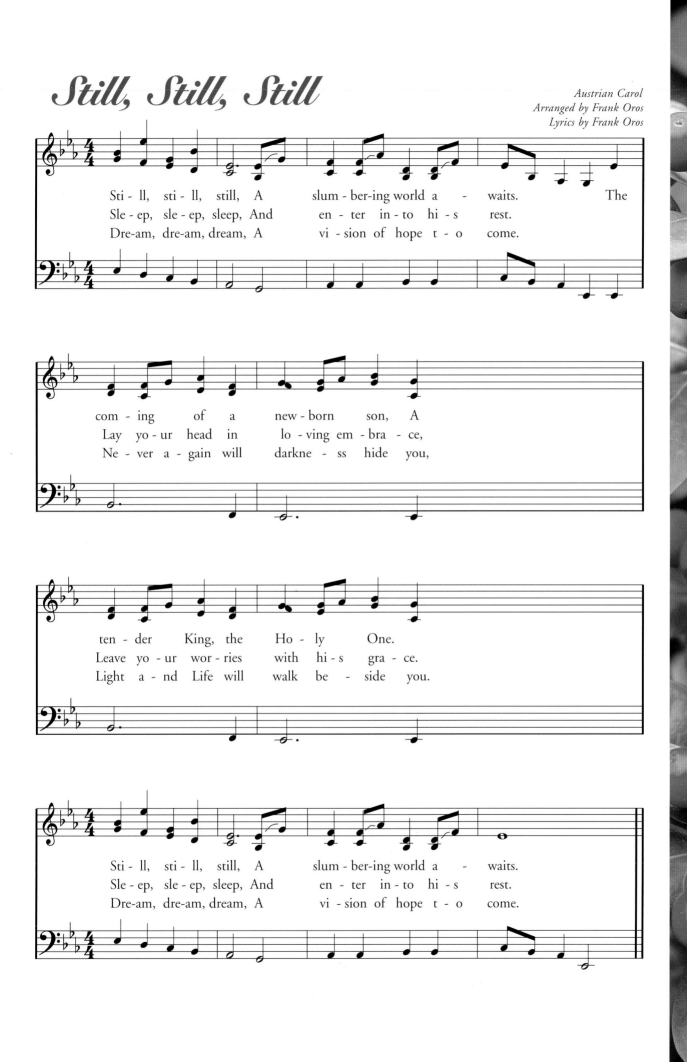

Sti - ll, sti - ll, still, A slum - ber-ing world a - waits. The
Sle - ep, sle - ep, sleep, And en - ter in - to hi - s rest.
Dre - am, dre-am, dream, A vi - sion of hope t - o come.

com - ing of a new - born son, A
Lay yo - ur head in lo - ving em - bra - ce,
Ne - ver a - gain will darkne - ss hide you,

ten - der King, the Ho - ly One.
Leave yo - ur wor - ries with hi - s gra - ce.
Light a - nd Life will walk be - side you.

Sti - ll, sti - ll, still, A slum - ber-ing world a - waits.
Sle - ep, sle - ep, sleep, And en - ter in - to hi - s rest.
Dre - am, dre-am, dream, A vi - sion of hope t - o come.

Ice water spring shelter

Belle Meade

Known as the "Queen of the Tennessee Plantations," Nashville's Belle Meade was once a world-renowned thoroughbred stud farm and nursery. At the center of the 5,000-acre plantation stood the grand 1853 Greek revival mansion, home to the Harding and Jackson families.

At a great plantation such as Belle Meade, preparation for the holiday season started many weeks prior to Christmas. It usually began with the annual hog slaughter early in December, when as much as 17,000 pounds of pork would be cut, salted, and smoked. When the fall harvest and winter planting were completed, there was time to celebrate, with social events, parties, balls, and weddings. It was during the Christmas season of 1868 that General William Hicks Jackson married Selene Harding, granddaughter of the founder of Belle Meade, and the two families were joined.

Then, as now, Christmas was a time for feasting and gift giving. Plantation records show that in 1879 the Jacksons gave their young daughter Selene a doll, which she named Louise. Young William received an engine with a cowcatcher and bell, and baby sister Eunice received a tiny diamond ring. Later that day, in keeping with Southern tradition, the children shot off firecrackers and skyrockets.

In December of 1895, William and Selene, then young adults, held a holiday dance at Belle Meade, with the details carefully noted. The entrance hall was filled with garlands of holly and tropical plants, and towering potted palms were placed throughout the ground floor. The parlors were decorated in white, gold, and pink, with sprigs of mistletoe tied with pink ribbons hung over the doors and between the rooms. The dining room was done in green and white, crystal candelabra adorned the tables, and cut-glass vases filled with white carnations and narcissus graced the serving sideboards. At midnight the guests sat down to an elaborate supper and afterward they danced until the wee hours of the morning to a live orchestra.

Top: Belle Meade's front parlor, with docents costumed in 1895 evening wear

Bottom: Entry hall, looking into the library

In keeping with Belle Meade's nineteenth-century traditions, contemporary Christmas celebrations at the plantation are created around specific themes, such as "A Currier and

The nursery strung with the Cobweb Game—each child follows a different colored string to find a gift

Belle Meade
Dec. 5 1882

Dear Cris. Please bring me a saddle and bridle and a riding whip. Bring me a stocking full of candy and oranges and anything you want to. I will try to be a good boy.

William H. Jackson
8 years old.

Letter to "Chris" (Santa Claus) from eight-year-old William Harding Jackson
Tennessee State Library and Archives

Susannah McGavock Carter was a slave at Belle Meade Plantation who stayed on as a cook after the Civil War. Susannah was known for her syllabub, a punch often served at Christmas consisting of whipping cream, Madeira wine and other ingredients. On one occasion, famed bear hunter Davy Crockett visited Belle Meade and was served a cup of Susannah's syllabub. "Do you like it?" William Giles Harding (then owner of Belle Meade) asked. "Well, I don't know," answered Crockett. "I took a snap or two at it, but I reckon I missed it."

—Belle Meade Plantation

Ives Christmas" or "A Gay '90s Christmas." In 1997 the theme was "A Christmas Wedding at Belle Meade," recreating the 1868 wedding of Selene Harding and William Hicks Jackson. Dressed in formal period attire, docents guided visitors through the mansion, which was elaborately decorated according to careful historic research. Each year at Christmas, the staff at Belle Meade brings to life a different historic period—all are authentically recreated and all reflect the beauty of the holiday season.

The elliptical staircase, the Executive Mansion, Nashville

*Governor and Mrs. Donald Sundquist
with Ruby and Milly*

The Executive Mansion

Originally called "Far Hills" because of the stunning view it commands, the elegant Nashville mansion now occupied by Tennessee's first family was built in 1929 by William Ridley Wills. Purchased by the state in 1949, the mansion has been home to eight governors, and today is the residence of Governor Donald Sundquist and First Lady Martha Sundquist. This graceful Georgian colonial brick home is set on ten beautifully landscaped acres, complete with reflecting pool. The grounds have been designated as an arboretum. The first floor of the mansion is filled with furniture, art, and treasures that are significant to the state of Tennessee, including a fifteen-gallon silver punch bowl presented to the battleship U.S.S. Tennessee when it was commissioned in 1906.

Christmas decorations at the Executive Mansion are numerous but simple, utilizing the many varieties of native greenery found in Tennessee. In 1997 a small "baby's first tree," with an exquisite antique doll at the base, was added in the foyer in honor of the Sundquist's first grandchild. Perhaps most fascinating is the large collection of nativity scenes that

Mrs. Sundquist has collected over the years. She first began collecting them when the children were growing up in Shelbyville, and the collection now features more than fifty nativity scenes from all over the world, ranging from small and simple to large and ornate. Mrs. Sundquist's sentimental favorite is made of olive wood from Bethlehem. Another favorite is from Africa, where the Sundquists visited the Zulus.

Of Swedish descent, the Sundquists include ancestral traditions in their holiday celebrations. One of the most lavish parties held at the Executive Mansion during the Christmas season is the Santa Lucia Breakfast. Santa Lucia, actually an Italian martyr, has become synonymous with the Swedish celebration of Christmas. According to tradition, when Christian missionaries first arrived in Sweden, they attempted to explain the concept of Christian light emanating from the darkest night. To illustrate, they adapted the image of the pure, young Lucia with a wreath of candles on her head walking out of the darkness into the light. She carried a basket of breads, also symbolic of Christianity.

The Sundquists continue this holiday tradition, with the oldest daughter of the family assuming the role of Santa Lucia, Queen of Light, for the December 13 celebration. Dressed in a robe of white with the candle wreath on her head, she descends the dramatic elliptical staircase to the guests below, in the same way that Santa Lucia emerged from the darkness carrying bread. Santa Lucia buns, often called "Lucia Cats," are served to the guests along with many other Swedish specialties. For the private family celebration, Santa Lucia wakes up the family with coffee and coffee bread.

The holidays are a busy time for the first family. The first two weeks of December are spent preparing for the Santa Lucia Breakfast and sending out more than 8,000 holiday cards. In addition, the Sundquists host an annual Holiday Open House and numerous other parties. When all the public activities are over, Christmas week is family week for the Sundquists. All of the children, spouses, and granddaughter Gabrielle arrive home to celebrate with Don, Martha, and first dogs Milly and Ruby. In addition to shopping and gift wrapping, the family loves to play games, especially Uno and Clue, and all are avid readers. Martha is particularly fond of carols and collects books of holiday music. Her favorite carol is "When Christmas Morn is Dawning," but, she admits, "I only play the piano when nobody is around."

Christmas Eve dinner is traditionally Swedish, with Swedish meatballs, Swedish potato sausage, rye bread, lingonberries (fixed like cranberry sauce), and caraway cheese. After attending church services on Christmas morning, the family returns home to a traditional turkey dinner—with Milly and Ruby anxiously hoping for leftovers.

The oldest daughter represents Santa Lucia

The people of Tennessee are the warmest, most caring, family-oriented and hard-working people we have ever met. We're proud to be part of this state.

—MARTHA SUNDQUIST,
First Lady of Tennessee

Mrs. Sundquist's Zulu nativity scene

SWEDISH CARDAMOM COFFEE BREAD

Dough
2 packages active dry yeast
9 cups (approximately) all-purpose flour
½ cup sugar
2 teaspoons ground cardamom
Pinch of salt
2½ cups milk

½ cup butter or margarine (1 stick)
2 eggs, lightly beaten

Glaze
1 egg yolk
1 teaspoon water
4 tablespoons sugar
1 teaspoon cinnamon

In a large mixing bowl, or in the bowl of an electric mixer fitted with a dough hook, combine yeast, 1 cup flour, sugar, cardamom and salt. In a saucepan, combine milk and butter and cook on medium-high heat until butter melts. Let cool to lukewarm.

Pour milk mixture into yeast mixture and beat together well. Stir in eggs. Slowly add remaining flour to make a soft but workable dough. Cover with a cloth and let stand for about 10 minutes.

Turn dough out onto a floured board and knead for 5 to 10 minutes, or until it doesn't stick to your hands. Cover and let rise in a warm place for 1 hour. Punch down dough and divide into 4 sections.

Then divide each section into 3 equal parts—about 5 ounces each if you want to weigh them on a kitchen scale. Roll each part between your hands to make 12-inch-long strips. Braid three strips together, pinching the ends under. Repeat with the remaining strips, for a total of 4 braided loaves. Transfer loaves to lightly greased cookie sheets, fitting 2 loaves per sheet.

Make the glaze by beating the egg yolk and water together. Brush on the tops of the loaves. Combine the sugar and cinnamon and sprinkle on top. Let loaves rise, uncovered, for 45 minutes to 1 hour, or until they double in size (but don't let the braids split).

Preheat oven to 350°F. Bake loaves for 15 to 20 minutes, or until browned. Let cool before slicing. This coffee bread can also be made in advance and frozen.

Makes 4 large loaves

A Swedish Christmas feast

—MARTHA SUNDQUIST, *First Lady of Tennessee, Nashville*

LUCIA BUNS

Sweet Roll Dough
½ cup warm water
2 packages active dry yeast
3¼ cups sifted flour
1½ cups lukewarm milk
½ cup sugar
½ cup shortening
2 eggs
2 tablespoons boiling water

2 teaspoons salt
1 teaspoon powdered cooking saffron
1 small box of raisins
Beaten egg yolk to glaze

Quick White Icing
Confectioners' sugar
Cream or milk as needed

Pour warm water into a large mixing bowl and add yeast, stirring to dissolve. Add remaining sweet roll ingredients, except for raisins and egg yolk, and mix with a spoon until smooth. Add more flour as necessary to handle dough easily, mixing by hand.

Turn dough onto lightly floured board and knead until smooth and elastic (about 5 minutes, using more flour if necessary). Form dough into a large ball and set in a greased bowl. Cover with damp cloth and let rise in a warm place (85° F) until dough has doubled in size (about 1½ hours). Punch dough down and let rise again until almost doubled (about 30 minutes). Divide dough for easy handling.

To shape buns, roll dough out to a ¼-inch thickness. Cut in thin strips, approximately 4 inches long and ½ inch wide. Cross 2 strips to make an "X," then curl each end in to form a broken "8." Press 4 raisins into each bun and brush with egg yolk. Let rise 15 to 20 minutes.

Preheat oven to 400°F. Bake buns 10 to 12 minutes until golden brown. Make Quick White Icing by mixing together confectioners' sugar and milk until smooth. Dribble with icing while buns are still warm from the oven.

Yields 4 dozen buns　　　　**—MARTHA SUNDQUIST,** *First Lady of Tennessee, Nashville*

GRANDMOTHER SWANSON'S SWEDISH MEATBALLS

1 pound lean ground beef
½ pound ground pork
1½ cups soft bread crumbs
　(Zwieback toast works well)
3 tablespoons butter
½ cup chopped onion

1 egg
1 cup half-and-half, or as needed
1½ teaspoons salt
¼ teaspoon ground ginger
⅛ teaspoon ground nutmeg
⅛ teaspoon pepper

In a large bowl, combine ground beef and pork. Add bread crumbs and mix well. Melt 1 tablespoon butter in sauté pan and sauté onion until softened. Add onion and egg to meat, along with enough half-and-half to pull mixture together. Add spices and seasonings, mixing thoroughly. Form into 1½-inch balls. (If mixture is difficult to handle, chill first).

In a frying pan, heat the remaining 2 tablespoons butter (vegetable oil may be substituted) on medium-high heat, and brown meatballs on all sides, shaking pan so that they retain their round shape. Remove meatballs from pan as they brown. When all the meatballs are browned, lower heat and return them to the pan to finish cooking through.

Makes 36 meatballs　　　　**—MARTHA SUNDQUIST,** *First Lady of Tennessee, Nashville*

CHRISTMAS FUDGE

3 cups sugar

6 tablespoons cocoa

2 tablespoons butter, softened

1 cup milk

3 tablespoons white Karo syrup

1 ½ teaspoons vanilla extract

½ cup black walnuts or pecans (optional)

In a mixing bowl, mix together sugar and cocoa. Add butter, milk and Karo syrup. Boil over medium-high heat, stirring frequently, until a spoonful of mixture forms a soft ball when dropped in a cup of cold water.

Remove from heat and add vanilla. Beat by hand until crusty around the edges. Pour fudge into a 10 x 13-inch buttered pan and cool. Slice into 1-inch squares while slightly warm.

Makes approximately 36 squares

Mother made every Christmas recipe—including Christmas Fudge—from her 1923 LARKIN HOUSEWIVES COOKBOOK. Over the years we've adjusted the amounts of the ingredients.

—JUDY WARREN

—JUDY WARREN, *Greenbrier*

"BAD" BROWNIES

1 cup margarine or butter (2 sticks)

1 ¾ cups light brown sugar, packed

2 eggs

2 cups all-purpose flour

2 teaspoons baking powder

1 teaspoon vanilla extract

1 tablespoon instant coffee

½ teaspoon salt

1 cup chopped nuts

1 cup chocolate chips

1 cup Heath Bar Brickle

Preheat oven to 350°F.

Cream butter and sugar together. Mix in eggs, flour, baking powder, vanilla, coffee and salt. Stir in ½ cup each of the nuts, chocolate chips and brickle.

Grease a 9 x 13-inch pan with baking spray. Spread batter in pan and sprinkle top with remaining nuts, chips and brickle.

Bake for 25 minutes or until a toothpick comes out clean. When brownies have cooled, cut into squares.

Makes 12 brownies

This recipe is one of my family's favorite easy-to-make desserts.

—REBECCA MILLER WEEKS

—REBECCA MILLER WEEKS, *Brentwood*

SUGAR PLUMS

1 cup dates

1 cup figs

1 cup raisins

1 cup candied fruit

1 cup nuts (walnuts or pecans)

2 tablespoons lemon juice

Granulated sugar

In a food processor, grind fruits and nuts together. Mix in lemon juice. Shape into 1-inch balls, roll in sugar and serve.

Makes 4 dozen

—PHILA HACH, *Hachland Hills Inn, Clarksville*

YULE LOG

Chocolate Biscuit Sheet Cake

4 eggs, whole

4 eggs, separated

¾ cup sugar

2 tablespoons cake flour

2 tablespoons cocoa powder

1 tablespoon cornstarch

4 egg whites

½ cup sugar

In a mixing bowl, whip whole eggs, 4 egg yolks and sugar until foamy. In a separate bowl, sift together flour, cocoa powder and cornstarch.

In another bowl, whip 8 egg whites, gradually adding sugar until it forms soft peaks. Fold egg whites into the whole egg mixture, then fold in sifted ingredients. Do not overmix!

Spread on a sheet pan or a jelly roll pan. Bake for approximately 15 minutes, or until firm.

Chocolate Mousse

2 cups milk

3 ounces bittersweet chocolate, broken into small pieces

1 ounce unflavored gelatin

6 cups heavy cream

Bring milk to a boil in a pot, then switch off burner. Add chocolate and stir until it has all melted.

Mix the gelatin with water until a pastelike consistency. Melt the gelatin to a liquid over a hot water bath. While still warm, add the chocolate mixture. Cool mixture on an ice bath, stirring continuously, until chocolate mixture has reached room temperature.

In a mixing bowl, whip the heavy cream to soft peaks and fold thoroughly into chocolate mixture. Set aside in a cool place.

Brush the biscuit sheet cake with a simple syrup mixture (equal parts water and sugar, boiled to melt the sugar), or brush with a liquor such as rum or brandy. Spread mousse on the sheet cake, setting aside 2 cups for decoration. Roll up the biscuit sheet cake like a jelly roll and chill for several hours.

Remove from refrigerator and cut off the end pieces and set them on the roulade, like branches. Cover log with the rest of the mousse and make tree bark designs with a fork. Decorate with colored candies, powdered sugar, and chopped pistachios to make it look Christmassy. Enjoy!

Serves approximately 12

—**Chef Richard Gerst,** *Opryland Hotel, Nashville*

My mother made beautiful yule logs each year as gifts to close friends.

—**Catherine Clark,**
Franklin

Bǔchë de Noël traditional Yule log, created by chocolatier Jerome Savin, Bluff View Inn

ENGLISH TRIFLE

First Layer

1 3-ounce package strawberry Jell-O

2 10-ounce packages frozen strawberries,
   partially thawed
   (set aside several for garnish)

1 angel food cake, cubed

Second Layer

2 3-ounce packages instant vanilla pudding

3 cups milk

Third Layer

3 bananas, sliced

Lemon juice

Fourth Layer

1 16-ounce container Cool Whip

I like to serve English Trifle because it not only tastes good, but it's also pretty with the four different layers showing through the glass.

—HELEN NORMAND

First Layer Mix Jell-O (without adding water) together with strawberries and place in a 2-quart glass container. Add angel food cake cubes.

Second Layer Mix according to package directions. Pour on top of first layer.

Third Layer Dip sliced bananas in lemon juice to prevent them from discoloring, then arrange on top of second layer.

Fourth Layer Spread Cool Whip on top of third layer and garnish with strawberries. Refrigerate until needed.

Serves 8   **—HELEN NORMAND,** *Oak Ridge*

TENNESSEE STACK CAKE

1 cup sugar

1 cup butter (2 sticks), softened

1 cup molasses

2 eggs

6 cups all-purpose flour

1 tablespoon baking powder

1 teaspoon baking soda

1 teaspoon salt

½ teaspoon ground ginger

½ cup buttermilk

My Tennessee grandma, "Coo-Coo" Roberson, has an old-fashioned stack cake made when we arrive in Tennessee for the holidays. We gather in the kitchen, which smells of spices, and enjoy a hot cup of tea with a piece of Tennessee Stack Cake.

—TRACEY ELIZABETH WILLIAMS

Preheat oven to 450°F.

Cream sugar and butter together in a large mixing bowl. Beat in molasses. Add eggs one at a time, beating well after each addition. In a separate bowl, combine dry ingredients. Add to butter mixture, alternating with buttermilk.

Shape dough into 7 balls. On a well-floured surface, use a rolling pin to roll each ball out into a 9-inch circle. One at a time, place each layer in a greased, 9-inch skillet or greased, 9-inch cake pan. Bake each layer for 10 minutes, or until golden brown. (Clean and grease skillet after each use.) Cool the layers, then spread the top of each with Apple Filling and stack.

Apple Filling

1 pound dried apples

1 cup brown sugar, firmly packed

½ cup sugar

2 teaspoons ground cinnamon

½ teaspoon ground cloves

In a large saucepan, cover dried apples with water and cook over medium heat until tender. Mash the apples thoroughly, add sugars and spices and mix well. Cool filling thoroughly before spreading on cake layers.

Serves 10 to 12   **—TRACEY ELIZABETH WILLIAMS,** *Asheville, North Carolina*

NUTCRACKER SWEET

6 eggs, separated
1 cup sugar
¼ cup flour
1¼ teaspoons baking powder
1 teaspoon cinnamon
½ teaspoon ground cloves
2 tablespoons vegetable oil

1 tablespoon rum extract
1 cup finely chopped nuts
1 cup finely crushed graham crackers
  (about 12 crackers)
1 square unsweetened chocolate,
  grated (1 ounce)
1 chocolate bar (any flavor) for garnish

Preheat oven to 350°F.

In a large mixing bowl, beat egg whites until frothy. Gradually add ½ cup sugar and continue beating until white peaks form.

In a small mixing bowl, blend remaining ½ cup sugar with the flour, baking powder, cinnamon and cloves. Add egg yolks, oil and rum flavoring, and beat with hand-mixer for 1 minute on medium speed.

Add egg yolk mixture to the beaten whites, gradually folding with a rubber spatula until blended. Fold in nuts, graham cracker crumbs and unsweetened chocolate.

Line the bottoms of two 9 x 9 x 1½-inch layer cake pans with aluminum foil. Pour batter into pans, and bake for 30 to 35 minutes, or until no imprint remains when touched lightly with finger. When done, cool by immediately inverting the pans, resting the edges of the cake pans on other inverted pans.

When cooled completely, loosen with spatula. Then invert pans again, hit sharply, and the layers will drop out. Top each layer with a frosting of rum-flavored whipping cream.

Frosting
2 cups whipping cream
1½ cups confectioners' sugar, sifted
2 teaspoons rum extract

In a small bowl, beat cream until cream is stiff. Continue beating while adding confectioners' sugar. Fold in rum extract. Frost cake layers and garnish with grated chocolate bar.

Refrigerate cake 7 to 8 hours, or overnight. The cake becomes increasingly moist and mellow with refrigeration.

Serves 10 to 12   —**DR. WALT MURPHY,** *formerly of Nashville*

We usually had this for Dad's birthday in December, but its name makes it a Christmas recipe.
—**DR. WALT MURPHY**

COCONUT CAKE

Golden Layer Cake

½ cup shortening
  (oil may be substituted,
  using ½ cup oil, less 1 tablespoon)
2¼ cups sifted, unbleached flour
1½ cups sugar

3 teaspoons baking powder
1 teaspoon salt
1 cup milk
2 eggs
1½ teaspoons vanilla

Preheat oven to 350°F.

Stir shortening just to soften. Sift in flour, sugar, baking powder and salt. Add only
⅔ cup milk and mix until flour is dampened. Beat vigorously for 2 minutes. Add remaining
⅓ cup milk, eggs and vanilla. Beat vigorously for 2 minutes more.

Bake in two waxed paper–lined, 9-inch round cake pans for about 30 minutes, or until
golden brown and toothpick comes out clean. (I grease and flour the sides of the pans and
a few spots under the waxed paper to anchor it—so it doesn't slip when the batter is
poured—and the top of the waxed paper as well.)

Coconut Filling

⅔ cup evaporated milk
⅔ cup sugar
¼ cup butter or margarine
1 egg, lightly beaten

Dash of salt
1 teaspoon vanilla
1 cup flaked coconut
½ cup chopped pecans

In a saucepan, combine milk, sugar, butter, egg and salt. While stirring, cook over
medium-low heat until mixture thickens and begins to boil, about 12 to 15 minutes.
Remove from heat. Add vanilla, coconut and pecans. When cooled thoroughly, spread
the filling between the two layers of the Golden Layer Cake.

White Icing with Marshmallows

2 egg whites, unbeaten
5 tablespoons water
1½ cups sugar
⅛ teaspoon cream of tartar
Dash of salt
18 large marshmallows
1 teaspoon vanilla

In the top of a double boiler, mix together
egg whites, water, sugar and cream of tartar and
sprinkle with salt. Cook 8 minutes in double
boiler, beating continuously. Remove from heat.
Add marshmallows and cook 7 minutes longer,
again beating continuously. Remove from heat
and add vanilla. Frost the top and sides of the
cake while the icing is warm.

Serves 8 to 10

—JANE ELLEN HODGES, *Dayton*

*I wish I had my mother's cake
recipes to share, but they are long
lost. I do remember that for her
annual Christmas coconut cake,
we used fresh coconut that had
to be broken with a heavy ham-
mer, peeled, and hand shredded.
Our knuckles usually got nicked
pretty good.*

—NANCY WAGGENER KING,
formerly of Nashville

SPECIAL DELIVERY
by Nancy Waggener King, formerly of Nashville

Mom never made desserts, except for Christmas dinner, when she
would make a fruit cake and a coconut cake. She always made two
of each so she could send the extras to her father in West Tennessee.
Grandpa Stroud, a widower of many years, lived alone in Gleason,
which was so small it was just a "flag stop" along the railroad line.

My dad's life work was sorting mail on the overnight train from
Nashville to Memphis. With all the stopping at small towns and
flag stops to dispatch the mail, the trip took eight to ten hours.

Every year my mother made the extra cakes for Grandpa, and, with
each cake carefully packaged, my father carried them to work with
him. By pre-arrangement the cakes were handed off to someone in
Gleason, who would have them hand-carried to Grandpa. And
every year Grandpa Stroud got his cakes!

MAMA BURNETT'S APPLESAUCE CAKE

1 cup sugar
½ cup shortening
1 egg
1½ cups applesauce
1 cup nuts, chopped
1 cup raisins

1 teaspoon vanilla
2 scant cups flour
1 tablespoon cocoa
½ teaspoon cinnamon
¼ teaspoon ground cloves

Preheat oven to 300°F.

Cream sugar and shortening. Add unbeaten egg and mix well. Add applesauce, nuts, raisins and vanilla. Mix well. Sift together dry ingredients and gradually add to shortening mixture. Pour batter into a greased tube pan and bake for about 1½ hours, until a toothpick comes out clean.

Serves 10 to 12

—**WINIFRED ROSE,** *Signal Mountain*

This is my husband's grand-mother's recipe. Mama used a caramel frosting on the cake.

—**WINIFRED ROSE**

SPICY PUMPKIN AND MOLASSES PIE

3 eggs
2 cups canned pumpkin
1 cup milk
½ cup molasses
¼ cup sugar
2 teaspoons cinnamon

½ teaspoon ground nutmeg
½ teaspoon ground ginger
½ teaspoon salt
½ teaspoon vanilla
1 9-inch prepared pie shell

Preheat oven to 400°F.

Place eggs in a large bowl, saving ½ teaspoon of egg white. Add remaining ingredients and beat until smooth.

Brush the ½ teaspoon of egg white on the bottom of pie shell. Pour pumpkin mixture into pie shell. Line oven rack with foil (the filling can boil over) and bake approximately 50 minutes, or until center appears firm.

Serves 8 to 10

—**RAMONA "MRS. GRANDPA" JONES**
From the GRANDPA JONES FAMILY COOKBOOK

I have little pecan Santa pigs that I made many years ago. We decorate a Christmas tree near the cashier's stand with them, along with gum balls sprayed silver and gold. We've been doing this for about eighteen years now, and people have come to expect it.

—**JANET BROWN,**
Leonard's Barbecue, Memphis

PECAN, CRANBERRY AND ORANGE TART

1 pie crust dough
1 cup sugar
1 cup corn syrup
2 cups toasted pecans

1 cup dried cranberries
2 oranges, zested
3 eggs

Preheat oven to 350°F.

Prepare your favorite simple pie dough and place in greased and floured tart mold. In a bowl, mix all remaining ingredients together.

Partially bake crust for 10 minutes. Remove from oven and add filling. Reduce heat to 300°F and continue baking for another 30 minutes, until firm when gently shaken. Let cool before serving.

Serves 8

—**EXECUTIVE CHEF BRAD GRAFTON,** *Bluff View Art District, Chattanooga*

Tennessee Chess Pie

Vanilla Layer

1 ¼ cups white sugar

½ cup butter, melted

¼ cup buttermilk

2 tablespoons cornmeal

¼ teaspoon salt

1 orange, zested

2 tablespoons vanilla

1 tablespoon Triple Sec liqueur

⅛ teaspoon nutmeg

Chocolate Layers

6 squares bitter chocolate

¾ cup butter

8 eggs

2½ cups white sugar

¼ cup all-purpose flour

½ teaspoon salt

¼ cup heavy cream

2 teaspoons vanilla

2 tablespoons dark rum

3   9-inch pie shells

Using your favorite pie dough recipe, roll dough to a ⅛-inch thickness and line three lightly greased 9 x 1-inch cake pans. Prick the dough with a fork to allow steam to escape. Place parchment paper on top of the dough, weighting it down with dried beans or pie weights. Preheat oven to 375°F, then parbake pie shells for 20 minutes until golden brown. Let cool slightly, remove parchment paper, then let cool completely.

This pie has three layers, two chocolate and one vanilla. To make the vanilla layer, beat eggs with a mixer until smooth. Add sugar and beat for 2 minutes. Stir in butter, buttermilk, cornmeal and salt. Stir for 1 minute, or until smooth. Add orange zest, vanilla, Triple Sec and nutmeg.

To make the chocolate layers, melt chocolate and butter together in a double boiler over low heat. In a large bowl, beat eggs with a mixer until smooth. In a separate bowl, combine sugar, flour and salt, then stir into eggs. Stir in cream and chocolate mixture. Add vanilla and rum.

Pour all of the vanilla filling into one parbaked pie shell. Divide the chocolate filling between the remaining two shells. Preheat oven to 425°F. Place pies in oven and immediately reduce temperature to 325°F. Bake for 45 minutes, or until pie filling is set. Let layers cool completely before assembling.

To assemble the pie, remove the layers from the cake pans by inverting onto cookie sheet covered with parchment or waxed paper. Stack layers on top of each other, with the vanilla layer in the middle. You may have to trim some pieces of the side crust for the layers to stack neatly. If desired, you can brush a layer of sugar syrup flavored with rum or Triple Sec between the layers.

Serves 12 to 16

— **CHEF JOHN FLEER,** *The Inn at Blackberry Farm, Walland*

*Christmas pies on a banquet table,
the annual Fort Louden Christmas feast*

FRUIT COBBLER

1 cup flour
2 teaspoons baking powder
Dash of salt
1 ¾ cups sugar

1 ½ cup milk
½ cup butter or margarine (1 stick)
1 16-ounce can peaches with juice (You can also use blackberries or other kinds of fruit.)

Preheat oven to 350°F.

In a mixing bowl, sift together flour, baking powder, salt and 1 cup of sugar. Add milk and mix well. Melt butter in the oven in a 2-quart casserole dish. Add the batter to the casserole dish, but do not mix the batter and butter together.

On the stove, heat the fruit with the remaining ¾ cup of sugar. Pour fruit over batter and bake uncovered for 50 minutes, or until golden brown and slightly bubbly. Cool to serve.

Serves 16

—LINDA WISE-TUCKER, *formerly of Miner Hill*

BOILED CUSTARD

3 cups whole milk
6 egg yolks
⅓ cup sugar

⅛ teaspoon salt
1 teaspoon vanilla

Scald milk in a pan and set aside. Place egg yolks in the top of double boiler and beat with a fork. Blend in sugar and salt, then slowly stir in milk. Set top of double boiler over simmering water.

Cook, stirring constantly until custard is thick enough to coat spoon. Remove from heat. Set top of double boiler into pan of cold water and cool quickly. Blend in vanilla. Pour into individual sherbet glasses and keep chilled until ready to use.

This boiled custard is unusual in that it doesn't "set." It stays rather liquid and at non-holiday times we often just pour it out of a pitcher to serve.

Yields 1 ½ pints

—PAT HILTON AND FRANCES BALDWIN, *Powell*

SNOW ICE CREAM

2 cups sugar
2 eggs
1 12-ounce can Eagle Brand evaporated milk

2 teaspoons vanilla extract
1 large pan of freshly fallen snow

Mix sugar, eggs, milk and vanilla in a container that will hold at least 1 gallon. Mix in the snow, adding just enough to achieve an ice cream consistency.

Another way to make snow ice cream is to pour a 12-ounce can of sweetened condensed milk in a bowl and add snow.

Serves approximately 10

—RAMONA "MRS. GRANDPA" JONES
From the GRANDPA JONES FAMILY COOKBOOK

We are now told that it's not good to eat snow, but come the season's first snowfall, I can't help thinking that "snow-cream" is a rare and wonderful treat.

—RAMONA "MRS. GRANDPA" JONES

FRUITCAKE COOKIES

1 cup nuts, broken into pieces

1 cup chopped dates

½ cup red candied cherries,
   cut into halves

½ cup green candied cherries,
   cut into halves

⅔ cup all-purpose flour

⅓ cup sugar

2 teaspoons baking powder

2 eggs, well beaten

1 teaspoon vanilla

Preheat oven to 450°F.

Mix nuts and fruit together in bowl. In a separate, larger bowl, combine flour, sugar and baking powder. Add eggs and mix well; add vanilla. Stir in the fruit and nuts, mixing well.

Drop dough by the teaspoonful onto a greased cookie sheet. Bake about 15 minutes, or until golden brown on top.

Makes 3 to 4 dozen cookies.

Variation: You can substitute ½ cup of dried pineapple or dried citrus for the green cherries. Adding 1 teaspoon of rum flavoring is another option.

—**ANNE M. AND WILLIAM ALLEN,** *Chattanooga*

This recipe was taken from a Cookie Swap article published in the CHATTANOOGA FREE PRESS some years ago. We have been making these for years in lieu of fruitcake.

—**ANNE M. AND
WILLIAM ALLEN**

JELLY ROLL

4 eggs

¾ cup sugar

¾ cup self-rising flour

1 teaspoon vanilla

1 16-ounce jar of your favorite jelly
   (I use grape)

Preheat oven to 375°F.

In a mixing bowl, beat eggs until stiff. Add sugar slowly while beating at medium speed, then slowly add flour and, finally, the vanilla. Pour batter into greased and floured 10 x 15 x 1-inch pan.

Bake for 8 to 10 minutes until golden brown. Remove pan from oven and lay a damp cloth over the cake; turn cake upside down, onto the cloth. Spread with jelly while cake is still hot. Starting from one end, roll the cake up, wrap the damp cloth around it so it holds its shape and secure with toothpicks. Refrigerate to cool. Remove cloth and cut into 1-inch slices.

Serves approximately 10

—**ADALENE WEESE BELL,** *Harrison*

When my family came to America from Italy, they went into the produce business, so we always had lots of fruit. At Christmas we made wonderful fruit-filled cookies with ground-up raisins, dates, figs, almonds, pecans, jelly, peach brandy, and all sorts of things. The family has been making them for more than ninety years now. Usually all the mothers would make them, but now it's only Aunt Annie, now ninety-three, who carries on the tradition. The kids and grandkids seem to know when she'll be baking and they stand around waiting for the cookies to be done. I am going to be the heir for the "secret" recipe.

—**MARY ALICE MASTELLONE,**
Memphis

Christmas tree farm,
Johnson County

The best Christmas
tradition is family!

—JOHNNA R. ROGERS,
Union City

When I see little kids in my Christmas tree lot, I tell them to look real close and they might see Santa Claus. If they tell me there is no Santa, I explain to them what Christmas is all about—that it's about giving from your heart without expecting anything in return.

—AL SMITH, *Hixson*

Tree decorated to feed winter
birds, Sam Houston Schoolhouse,
near Maryville

THE ONE-ARMED TREE MAN
by Bonnie Allin, Chattanooga

Going to get the Christmas tree is always an adventure, and for the last twelve years that adventure has become something special to us and our four sons. Actually, it was because of someone special—Al, the one-armed tree man.

That first year we all piled in the car and went to a corner tree lot in Chattanooga, ready to make a purchase. We ended up making friends as well. There was something different about Al and his wife, Edna. They didn't just sell trees; they gave the gift of Christmas along with those trees, and in doing so, they captured our hearts.

Al wasn't satisfied just to drag out trees and get it over with. He wanted to meet us, to know us, and to let us know that the meaning of Christmas is love. He quoted us a song about love and then he asked us for a Christmas present. He kneeled down next to each child, one by one, and asked for a hug. They hugged him right then and there, and from that moment on, he was our personal Christmas tree man.

Always cheerful, he never forgot our names, even though we sometimes only saw him once a year. After a couple of years we started baking him cookies and bringing our own little Christmas party to the tree lot to share with Al and Edna. Year after year, we have gone to see Al and have come away not only with a tree but also with the spirit of Christmas. As my children have grown, now my youngest son and I go to the lot. Every time we look at our Christmas tree we are reminded of the one-armed tree man named Al who has made a difference in our lives.

THE MEANING OF CHRISTMAS
by Al Smith, Hixson

My friends call me the "one-armed bandit" or sometimes, affectionately, Captain Hook. I'm not a native of Tennessee, but my wife, Edna, and I fell in love with the state thirty years ago when we moved to Hamlin County. We fell in love with the mountains, the scenery, and, most of all, the people. When I retired from the ministry, I just couldn't sit around, so I started umpiring. Needing something else to do, I decided to start selling Christmas trees. That was about thirteen years ago, and I've had so much fun that I plan to keep doing it until I can't any more.

Sometimes we trade a tree for meals from neighboring restaurants, anything from pizza to pancakes. When people buy a tree from me, I tell them all about it—what kind of tree it is and how to care for it. We're doing more than selling trees, we're making people happy.

I'll never forget when the Allin family started coming to my lot. They were special, different from most of the others. They came with their four little boys (not so little any more), and we got to know each other and to share our faith. It took them nearly an hour to pick out their Fraser fir, and we had such a good time that they didn't want to leave. They come year after year, but never just to buy a tree. They come for the fellowship— that's the joy of it.

There's a song that I like to recite that I think defines the meaning of Christmas—which is love. It goes something like this:

> *You can't hold it in your hand*
> *You can't see it with your eyes*
> *But like the wind it covers our land*
> *Strong enough to rule the heart of any man*
> *This thing called love.*
> *It can lift you up*
> *It can let you down*
> *It can take your world and spin it all around*
> *Ever since time, nothing's been found that's*
> *stronger than love.*

We decorate our tree with dozens of handmade ornaments—many of them Smoky Mountain crafts— and with fifty-year-old glass ornaments that have been handed down through my family. On top of the tree is an antique angel in a silver dress. When my husband and I were first married and didn't have much money, I made twenty old-fashioned clothespin ornaments, which have held up perfectly for twenty-five years. As much as possible we try to give gifts that are made in Tennessee.

—**Kathy Torgerson,** *Gray*
(Kathy Torgerson is the great-great-granddaughter of the only surviving daughter of the eleven-member Lewis family, who settled in the Greasy Cove region of Unicoi County in 1778. A band of Indians, mistaking the Lewises for another family, massacred the parents and seven children. The daughter was held hostage and later ransomed for a gun.)

Elegant Christmas tree, Memphis

At the Fontaine House in Memphis, there is a Christmas tree that hangs upside down in the entryway. It seems Queen Victoria had six children and she was afraid they would break the ornaments, so she had the tree hung from the ceiling after it was decorated. The Fontaine House continues this tradition. One year we took the children to hang ornaments before the tree was raised.

—**Michael and Ramona Fredman,** *Memphis*

We used to put up our tree on Christmas Eve, which always meant a trip to the store to replace icicles and angel's hair and burnt-out Christmas tree lights. I hoped Santa would come early, while we were gone, because surely I'd be able to talk my parents into letting me open my presents early.

—**Linda Wise-Tucker,** *formerly of Miner Hill*

THE ANGEL TREE

by Marilyn L. Harris, Tullahoma

Last year we decided that instead of having a Christmas tree, we would have an "Angel Tree." We purchased an angel ornament for each loved one who is no longer with us—family and friends who have passed away. We then took a picture of each angel and started an "Angel Photo Album." Under the angel's picture is the name of the person the angel represents and a favorite story about that person, along with his or her place on our family tree.

This year when we hung our angels on the tree, we told our favorite stories of each person. Retelling the stories keeps our loved ones' memories alive and also gives the younger generation a fond memory of them. Our Angel Tree has made Christmas a very happy occasion because we have so many friends and family members with us in spirit to celebrate the Christmas season.

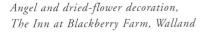

Angel and dried-flower decoration,
The Inn at Blackberry Farm, Walland

Every year I print a Christmas letter to mail to family and friends, summarizing what my family and I have done the past year. Some people think printed letters are too impersonal, but I think they are a wonderful way to keep in touch, because none of us has the time to write all the personal letters we would like.

—JANE ELLEN HODGES,
Dayton

I remember my Daddy going out Christmas Eve day to get our Christmas tree, so I don't usually rush to put my tree up like others do. Since my name is Lamb, a number of ornaments on the tree have to do with lambs. Every ornament on the tree has special significance, and I like to think of their meaning as I put them on the tree each year. I also have a bear collection and beautiful old dolls that go under the tree.

—LINDA TIPTON LAMB, Maryville

 My mother, widowed at age thirty-four, raised four children. She always decorated for Christmas after Thanksgiving dinner. My youngest sister and her son continue the tradition.

—SARAH MOODY STINNETT, *Charleston*

Ribbons and bows

CHRISTMAS IN JULY
by Shelia Wilson, South Pittsburg

My most memorable Christmas was in 1992. It was the best Christmas, the worst
Christmas, and it was in July! Mama had had a heart attack and was in intensive care.
We got word and rushed straight home from our vacation. The doctors said Mama
needed major surgery. She told the doctors she'd be back in two weeks.

Once at home, Mama wanted to put up her Christmas tree and have Christmas in July.
I got out the tree and put it up where she could see it from her bed. Mama gave us all
Christmas gifts that July, giving us money and telling us to spend it on something we
really wanted.

The two weeks went by all too quickly and soon it was time to go back to the hospital.
We put on brave faces and took off for Chattanooga. All the family came to the hospital.
Mama made it through the surgery and our Christmas really had come in July, because
we got to keep Mama with us.

Preparing for a snowball fight

Left: Town square and
Christmas tree, Collierville
Below: Lobby of the Cotton
Exchange, Memphis

*Christmas holidays always began
with us stringing lights around
the front porch posts and windows. After dark our house was
visible from a mile away. I knew
Santa wouldn't have a problem
finding us.*

—LINDA WISE-TUCKER,
formerly of Miner Hill

The Tullahoma Tree

by Verne and Frank Ernst,
formerly of Tullahoma

For more than fifty years a special Norwegian
spruce has graced the town of Tullahoma. When
Aunt Taters and Uncle Ben Wilkins (great-great-
grandson of President Benjamin Harrison, reportedly
the first president with a decorated Christmas tree on the White House lawn) started decorating the little tree on their lawn in 1946, they only needed a few lights. Year after year,
as the little tree grew, they kept adding more. Pretty soon people in town began expecting
the tree to be lighted, and they were never disappointed. Every year, except for a few years
when Americans were conserving energy, Uncle Ben and Aunt Taters lit the tree just
before the annual Christmas parade.

Uncle Ben died in 1975 and Aunt Taters in 1978, and folks not only mourned the loss
of their friends, but also the passing of the Christmas tree lighting tradition. But they
needn't have worried. Subsequent owners of the property, along with family members and
local business interests, have kept lighting the tree as a tribute to the Tullahoma couple
who brought Christmas joy to so many. Now sixty feet tall, the Norwegian spruce still
delights thousands of people each year.

Besides putting up a tree, my holiday
tradition has been to place candles
in the windows and decorate my two
front doors, as I live on the intersec-
tion of two main roads.

—JANE ELLEN HODGES, Dayton

Phila Hach

A TENNESSEE LADY AT CHRISTMAS

She smiles and laughs with sparkling eyes. With her snow-white hair piled up in a bun and a ruffled, calico apron covering her puff-sleeved country dress, she looks like the perfect grandma from a storybook. And she bakes the most wonderful Christmas cookies for her guests and many friends who visit her Hachland Hill Inn in Clarksville. Phila Hach is truly an extraordinary woman.

Sitting in front of a roaring fire in Phila's comfortable parlor, munching on cookies, and drinking hot cider while listening to her life story, one begins to understand just how truly extraordinary she is. Among her numerous accomplishments, she is a highly educated nutritionist with a degree from Vanderbilt University, a nationally recognized chef, a cookbook author seven times over, and a world traveler.

It was on a flight to Paris as an international flight attendant for American Airlines in the 1940s that Phila first met Adolf Hach, the dashing gentleman who would become her husband. Although she doesn't remember that first meeting, he recognized her several years later on TV. Phila was the star of the first cooking show in the South, a daily thirty-minute program called "Kitchen Kollege," in which she not only cooked, but did the commercials as well. Adolf made an effort to find her and two years later they were married. They established the Hachland Hill Inn and started a family.

They added onto their little piece of "Tennessee Heaven" as they found and moved several old log cabins onto their property. Their most interesting acquisition was the 1790 cabin in which Andrew Jackson lived while the Hermitage was being built. Each cabin was lovingly restored and furnished with Phila's eclectic collection of antiques and handmade crafts given to her by family, friends, and guests.

Cotton bolls, often used in Christmas decorations in West Tennessee

A popular place for weddings and parties, Hachland Hill Inn is decorated completely in red and green for the holidays. Two hundred red poinsettias are brought in. Evergreen garlands and sprigs of greenery are everywhere, many tied with large red bows. Two giant trees outside the front door supply an abundance of holly leaves with glossy red berries.

Christmas would not be complete without Phila's "cookie village." After Christmas her grandchildren nibble on the pieces until they are all gone, often not until after New Year's. Phila also makes cookies to hang on the Christmas tree, along with the dozens of handmade ornaments given to her by guests of the inn. For many years she had a charming policy that required guests who brought an ornament for her tree to take one off the tree for themselves. "You wouldn't believe my collection!" she laughs. "I have the most unusual array of Christmas ornaments from all over the world."

"Down in the Mississippi River delta, people decorate with cotton bolls, sometimes painting the outer shell," she explains. "Some even take the cotton out and insert little figures, perhaps a nativity scene. The further you go up the Tennessee River, the more pine cones and hawthorn berries are used." She recalls seeing simple but beautiful miniature trees made out of pine cones in East Tennessee and even cattails dipped in silver paint and hung on the tree with thistles and sycamore balls.

As optimistic as she is spirited, Phila believes that people are starting to turn against the commercialism of Christmas. "I think people are relearning the simple meaning of Christmas," says Phila. "I think people are starting to see how much love they can spend rather than how much money. It's such a simple concept."

Wherever Phila Hach is, there is love all around. Perhaps that is the reason why she counts her good friends in the thousands. The Christmas spirit lasts all year round at Hachland Hill Inn—Phila Hach wouldn't have it any other way.

SANTA ADOLF
by Phila Hach, Hachland Hill Inn, Clarksville

One year I was busily decorating the inn for Christmas while two little children were here with their mother. I had asked my husband, Adolf, to go out and pick up some packages that I had had wrapped. He left dressed in his customary red blazer and soon returned with his arms loaded with presents. The children excitedly insisted to their mother that they had just seen Santa Claus.

I quickly went and found Adolf, who was a tall man with lovely white hair and a full beard. He returned to the children, and without saying a word, beckoned them to him. Sitting one on each knee, he spoke in a deep, raspy voice, the result of recent throat surgery. "Now children," he said, "what do you want Santa to bring you for Christmas?" The little boy punched his sister in the arm and said, "See, I told you it was Santa Claus. He doesn't even talk like real people." We had some good laughs about that one.

During the holidays we have a family group picture taken to compare the growth of grandchildren from year to year.

—ANNE AND WILLIAM ALLEN, *Chattanooga*

Paper ornaments, Maryville

When we were little, my parents made us wait until our grandparents arrived before we could go into the den where the Christmas tree was. They wanted our grandparents to be there to see our delight at the things Santa brought.

—ELIZABETH ANN JOHNSON, *Athens*

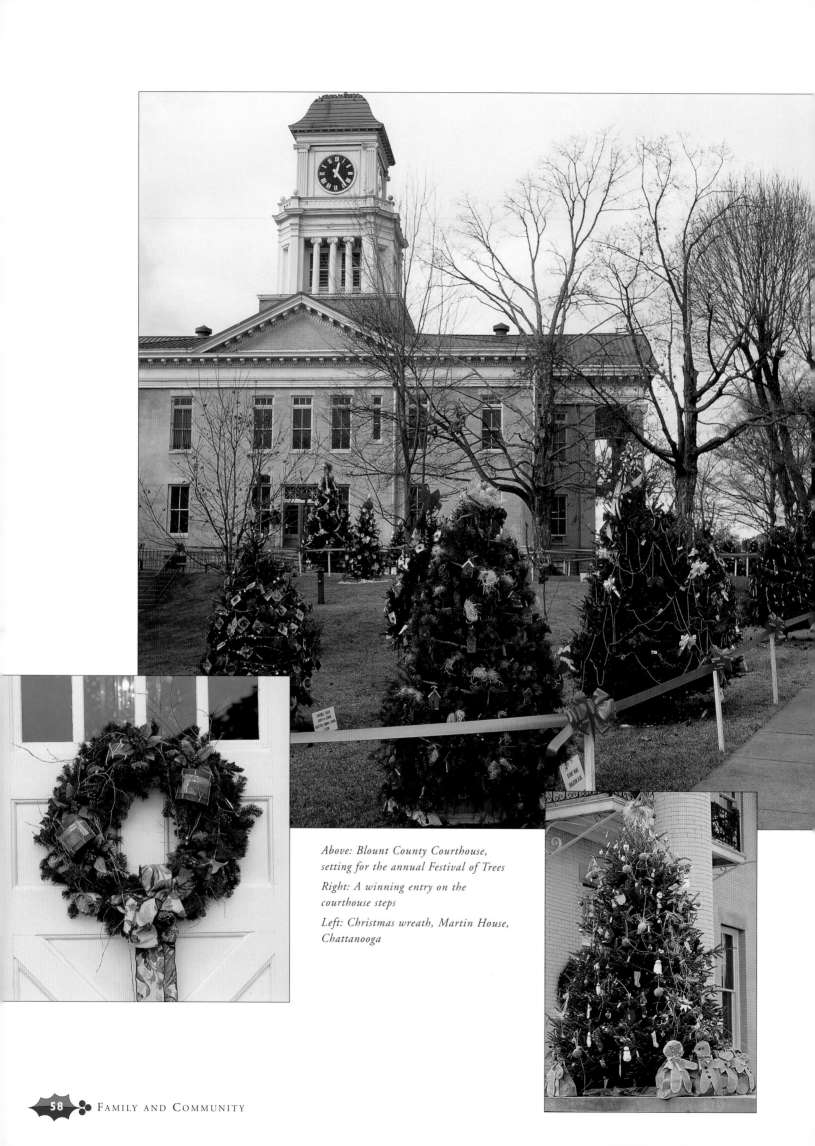

Above: Blount County Courthouse, setting for the annual Festival of Trees

Right: A winning entry on the courthouse steps

Left: Christmas wreath, Martin House, Chattanooga

GRANDMOTHER'S CHRISTMAS QUILT

by John Rice Irwin

When I began to develop a book on Appalachian quilts, I had the idea of the quilt as a vehicle to examine peoples' lives. One day my dad said, "You ought to put your grandmother's Christmas quilt in there." I had never heard of Grandmother's Christmas quilt, but I discovered it was owned by my uncle and I borrowed it from him.

Glenn G. Irwin, John Rice Irwin's father, with the Christmas quilt

My grandmother was one of eleven children. When her only sister moved to Oklahoma, Grandmother had to take over the household chores. She was just a young girl, but a prodigious worker: cooking, sewing, cleaning, slicing the meat in the smokehouse—doing all the household work for her large family.

I remember waking up in the morning and hearing her in the kitchen making biscuits and slicing ham, whistling while she worked. She was a very friendly and lovable lady, and we got along just great. She would cook whatever I brought back from hunting, making squirrel soup or whatever.

I never knew Grandmother had any artistic attributes or inclinations because everything she had done had always been work. But in the late 1890s she made a crazy quilt, filling it with strips of material and covering it with little images that meant a lot to her, such as a Jew's harp and a fiddle (she loved music), chickens (the only money she could call her own was from raising chickens and selling eggs), and the names of girlfriends. She loved to ride a horse and the quilt had a horse with a side saddle. All those little depictions were so real to her.

Down on the bottom of the quilt, in the corner, were the most dramatic words that I've ever read: "Remember Me." It was almost as though she was crying out in those two words she had embroidered there. It suddenly occurred to me that when she married she had lost her maiden name. When people talked about the farm it was always John Irwin's farm; when they referred to the kids it was Uncle John Irwin's children. She wasn't unhappy with those circumstances. But it was so dramatic to see those small words, asking for recognition.

Grandmother never called it a Christmas quilt, but every year she would bring it out a few days before Christmas. Everyone was carefully admonished not to sit on it, but it brightened and livened up the room. After Christmas, it was carefully folded and put back in the cedar chest, where it stayed for the rest of the year.

I am now the proud owner of the Christmas quilt, and Grandmother Irwin needn't worry. She will be remembered.

When our children were younger, my mother made stockings for them from a quilt my great-grandmother made. I have a lot of family quilts and like to use them to decorate.

—KATHY TORGERSON, *Gray*

*Oposite: Tennessee front porch
and wreath, Franklin*

*Left: Decorated drive, Lookout
Mountain*

Both our children are married now and have their own
families. They come to our house on Thanksgiving, and for
Christmas we alternate between our son's house one year
and our daughter's the next. We celebrate our family
Christmas the weekend before, so that our children can
have their own Christmas at home with their kids.

—**ANNE AND WILLIAM ALLEN,** *Chattanooga*

Abolitionist House, Jonesborough

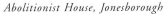

Historic Jonesborough

We host our annual "Family Jubilee" on December 23—
an elegant party for our neighbors and close friends,
including children of all ages. A surprise visit by Santa
Claus highlights the evening.

—**PATTY AND JOHN HOLBROOK,** *Johnson City*

My mother-in-law gives each of her three sons' families a pot and an amaryllis bulb every Christmas. The children love to watch the plant's rapid growth and bloom.

—PATTY AND JOHN HOLBROOK, *Johnson City*

We still hang stockings and are just as happy to get nuts, oranges, and candy canes in them. When my twin sister and I were younger, we would go rooting through my Dad's sock drawer to find that special stocking.

—LINDA TIPTON LAMB, *Maryville*

Above: Christmas tree at the Bluff View Inn, Chattanooga

Left: Mantle of the Great House, Museum of Appalachia, Norris

Bluff View Art District

Like a phoenix rising, a once-prosperous Chattanooga neighborhood has risen again, now as the highly acclaimed Bluff View Art District. Situated on the bluffs overlooking the Tennessee River, the Bluff View Art District has grown into a bustling and diverse art community—a success story in urban development.

Once home to prestigious Chattanooga families, such as the Maclellans, Newells, Thompsons, and Martins, the neighborhood boasted many old mansions and stately homes, some in disrepair. In 1993, local physician Dr. Charles Portera and his wife, Mary, purchased their first property, which they reno- vated and turned into the River Gallery. As other properties became available, the Porteras and members of their family began to develop the area with a unique vision in mind. One by one, the old buildings were carefully restored and renovated, gradually assuming new identities as restaurants, a banquet hall, bed and breakfasts, shops, and art galleries featuring the works of highly acclaimed local, regional, and international artists.

The redevelopment project was strongly influenced by both European and New Orleans styles of architecture. Wrought-iron gates open onto charming cobblestone walks. Fountains splash in hidden courtyards. Many windows are handcrafted with beveled, stained, or leaded glass. Antique doors, salvaged banisters, and old wood beams are incorpo- rated into the buildings whenever possible, creating a union of both the old and the new. The Porteras' strong commitment to excellence is nowhere more evident than in the lovely Sculpture Garden, where permanent and exhibited works by renowned sculptors are displayed for the public to enjoy while strolling through the tranquil garden setting.

Bluff View Inn, located atop scenic bluffs overlooking Tennessee River, Chattanooga

Accessible from the Tennessee Riverwalk via the Walnut Street Pedestrian Bridge, and just across from the Hunter Museum of American Art, the Bluff View Art District fills the senses with visual and culinary delights during the Christmas season. Nearly every doorway invites entrance, enticing you inside to observe artists at work or sample the day's fresh offerings. There is an eclectic assortment of restaurants and cafes boasting highly credentialed chefs who prepare an international range of cuisines. The district's French chef prepares fabulous pastries daily. Stop by the Chocolate Kitchen to see chocolate Santas being made, or visit The Bakery to watch an elaborate gingerbread village being built. Just as the baker care- fully plans and executes this confectionary village, so too was the Bluff View Art District artfully conceived and crafted. It is a work of art in itself.

Overleaf: Fall Creek Falls gorge

Opryland Hotel, Nashville

Christmas tree in the conservatory

Opryland USA
"A COUNTRY CHRISTMAS"

Opryland USA—the name that evokes so many bright images associated with Nashville and country music—offers an interesting experience at any time of the year, but when Christmas comes, Opryland gets even brighter. From historic Ryman Auditorium to the spectacular Opryland Hotel, every location and event is glittering with the excitement of the season.

The Ryman Auditorium has more than 100 years of history (some of it rather checkered) to its credit, beginning with a Gospel Tabernacle, which riverboat Captain Thomas Green Ryman built as a place for great religious services after he was converted in a tent meeting. Later incarnations of the building included a convention hall; an opera, symphony, and ballet stage; a movie and vaudeville house; and, finally, the home of the radio show called Grand Ole Opry.

The Grand Ole Opry was born in 1925 as the Barn Dance on station WSM-AM. It moved from location to location as it rapidly grew, finally ending up in the Ryman Auditorium in 1943, where it remained until 1974. It then moved to the new 4,400-seat Grand Ole Opry House, which has become the centerpiece of country music entertainment. On Friday and Saturday nights during the holidays, both the Ryman Auditorium and the Grand Ole Opry House feature music of the season, ranging from the Nashville Symphony and Chorus' "Messiah" to performances and tapings of Christmas shows on TNN: The Nashville Network.

Since its beginnings in 1984, "A Country Christmas" has become one of the premier holiday attractions in the nation, focusing on the fabulous Opryland Hotel, a massive complex with nearly 3,000 rooms. For the months of November and December, hotel guests and tens of thousands of holiday visitors enter the grounds through a squad of sixteen neon Nutcracker Suite toy soldiers. An astonishing 2,200,000 Christmas lights shine on virtually every tree, bush, fence, and building. A seven-member horticultural crew begins stringing lights in July to assure completion by November.

As spectacular as the exterior of the hotel is, the interior is even more dazzling. Three indoor gardens, called "interiorscapes," comprise a total of nine acres, all fantastically decorated. The newest of these, the Delta, features a fifty-foot-tall decorated Christmas tree, five cold-air balloons, and a fourteen-foot-wide wreath under a massive 650-ton sparkling glass roof that rises to a height of 150 feet. Meandering leisurely through the gardens are festive flatboats carrying up to twenty-five passengers along the quarter-mile Delta River. The Delta is now the location of the hotel's long-time tradition "Ceremony of the Yule Log," in which staffers don medieval costumes and portray villagers who banish the woes of the year and enlist guests in the singing of carols. Before and after the ceremony, a fountain shoots ninety-seven jets of water eighty-five feet into the air.

In the Conservatory garden more than 10,000 tropical plants grow beneath another glass roof. A third giant roof covers the Cascades, where three waterfalls cascade over a forty-foot mountain into a 12,500 square-foot lake. During the holidays, the computer-controlled "Dancing Waters" laser fountain show takes place to the sounds of Christmas music.

To complete the Opryland Hotel's holiday offering is a Country Christmas Art, Antique, and Craft Fair and a major musical production held in the 55,270-square-foot Delta Ballroom. In addition to the many Christmas activities at Opryland USA, there are also special holiday-themed cruises on the General Jackson showboat as it cruises down the Cumberland River in Victorian splendor.

Poinsettia tree in the lobby

Living in Nashville meant seeing country music stars frequently, even offstage. One sure way to spot a few was to go over to the Opryland Hotel on Thanksgiving weekend. After driving through the massive light display surrounding the hotel, we would stroll through the hotel to see the Christmas decorations in the conservatory. Almost inevitably we would spot a romantic couple or parents with small children who looked familiar, only to realize that they were country artists.

—**DR. WALT MURPHY,**
formerly of Nashville

STREUSEL COFFEE CAKE

Streusel
½ cup granulated sugar
½ cup chopped pecans
2 tablespoons flour
2 tablespoons oil
2 teaspoons cinnamon

Cake
¼ cup butter or margarine, softened
¾ cup sugar
1 egg
1½ cups flour
¾ cup milk
2 teaspoons baking powder
½ teaspoon salt

Preheat oven to 350°F.

In a mixing bowl, combine all streusel ingredients and mix with a fork. Set aside.

To make the cake, cream butter and sugar until soft and creamy. Mix in egg. Add milk and flour alternately. Stir in baking powder and salt.

Pour half the batter into a greased and floured 9 x 9-inch glass pan. Cover with half of the streusel mixture. Add remaining batter and cover with rest of streusel. (You can double the amount of streusel for extra richness.)

Bake approximately 30 minutes, or until toothpick inserted in center comes out clean.

Serves 9 to 12   **—BONNIE ALLIN,** *Chattanooga*

I was given this recipe by a missionary from Brazil when I was nine years old, and I have made it ever since.

—BONNIE ALLIN

For breakfast we have a birthday coffee cake to celebrate Jesus's birthday.

—CATHERINE CLARK, *Franklin*

CHRISTMAS STOLLEN

1⅓ cups flour
1⅓ sticks butter, softened
¾ cup small curd cottage cheese
4 tablespoons butter, melted
1 cup light brown sugar
1 cup shredded coconut

½ cup chopped pecans
¾ teaspoon cinnamon
¼ teaspoon nutmeg

Glaze
¼ cup confectioners' sugar
¼ cup water

In a mixing bowl, combine flour, butter and cottage cheese; cover and refrigerate overnight.

Knead dough, then roll out on floured board into large rectangle, approximately 10 x 18 inches, making the dough as thin as possible. Brush dough with melted butter.

In a bowl, mix together brown sugar, coconut, pecans, cinnamon and nutmeg, then sprinkle over buttered dough. Roll dough up lengthwise. Place on a lightly greased cookie sheet and shape into a wreath. Cut 5 diagonal slashes on top of the dough.

Preheat oven to 350°F. Bake for 35 to 40 minutes until light brown on top. Make a glaze of equal parts confectioners' sugar and water, stirring until smooth. Drizzle stollen with glaze while it is still warm from the oven.

Serves 12   **—SARAH YANN,** *Hermitage*

Every year my mother made this pastry-like stollen, which we would have Christmas morning with coffee or eggnog. Now that I am married and have three children, I carry on the same tradition. I often double the recipe to give the extra to a friend along with the recipe.

—SARAH YANN

Christmas feast, Opryland Hotel, Nashville

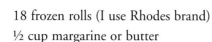

PAULA'S STICKY BUNS

18 frozen rolls (I use Rhodes brand)
½ cup margarine or butter
½ cup light brown sugar

1 teaspoon cinnamon
1 3½-ounce package butterscotch
  pudding mix (not instant)

Arrange the frozen rolls in a bundt pan sprayed with cooking oil. In a saucepan, melt margarine over medium heat; stir in brown sugar and cinnamon until sugar is dissolved. Pour over rolls and sprinkle pudding mix on top. Cover with a towel and let rise overnight at room temperature.

Preheat oven to 375°F. Bake for 30 minutes, covered with foil for the first 15 minutes. It is wise to put a cookie sheet underneath the bundt pan to catch drips.

Invert bundt pan over a large plate and lift pan. A pretty ooey-gooey ring of buns should happen! Buns are best served while still warm, as the glaze hardens when it cools.

Serves 12 to 18

—**LEE AGUILERA**, *Nashville*

We only use this recipe on special occasions. It has become a part of our Christmas tradition every year and is a comfort food when we are not able to be home for the holidays. This breakfast treat is not only tasty, but it also represents good times and family togetherness.

—**LEE AGUILERA**

PANCAKES

¾ cup self-rising flour, sifted
3 tablespoons sugar
1 large egg

½ cup milk
⅓ cup cooking oil

In a mixing bowl, combine flour and sugar. Separate egg, reserving yolk in large bowl. In a smaller bowl, beat egg white until it peaks softly.

Add milk to yolk and beat until foamy. Continue beating while adding oil, then add the flour mixture, beating until well blended. Add a little milk if a thinner consistency is required. Fold in egg white.

Lightly oil griddle and cook pancakes until golden brown.

Serves 4 hungry people

—**RICHARD W. BELL, SR.**, *Harrison*

This is a recipe that I developed over the years. It wouldn't be Christmas morning without these pancakes for breakfast.

—**RICHARD W. BELL, SR.**

CHOCOLATE GRAVY
CIVIL WAR RECIPE

1 cup water
2 cups sugar
2 tablespoons cocoa

2 heaping tablespoons flour
  (self-rising makes it lighter)
¼ cup butter

In a sauce pan, bring water to a boil. In a mixing bowl, combine sugar, cocoa and flour, making sure all lumps are broken up. Quickly stir sugar mixture into boiling water and whip with wire whisk.

Cook 5 to 8 minutes over medium heat, stirring occasionally, until the mixture comes to a slow boil and the gravy thickens. Add butter, keeping on medium heat and stirring until melted. Serve over hot biscuits.

Serves 6 to 8

—**PHILA HACH**, *Hachland Hill Inn, Clarksville*

The long-standing tradition in our family has always been to have Christmas morning at Grandma and Grandpa's house. We always had a big breakfast—biscuits with cheese slices and homemade preserves, sausages, bacon, eggs, and fried chicken. Grandma raised chickens, and on Christmas morning she would go out and wring the necks of a couple of chickens and have them ready for breakfast. If you have never eaten a chicken that fresh, you don't know what you are missing!

—**LINDA SANDERS**, *Columbia*

COUNTRY BREAKFAST CUSTARD

2 cups milk

2 teaspoons cinnamon

½ cup sugar

2 tablespoons cornstarch

1 tablespoon flour

Dash of salt and pepper

3 eggs, separated

1 tablespoon butter

1 teaspoon vanilla

Bread crumbs

In a saucepan, boil 1 cup milk and cinnamon. Set aside. In a mixing bowl, combine the other cup of milk (cold) with sugar, cornstarch, flour, salt and pepper.

Beat egg yolks and stir into flour mixture, then add in milk mixture. Cook in double boiler over medium heat, stirring until thick.

Remove from heat and add butter and vanilla. Pour custard into a greased, 2-quart glass casserole and refrigerate until firm.

Cut into 2-inch squares, roll in lightly beaten egg whites, dredge in bread crumbs and fry on both sides until golden brown. Grandmother used to like the grease, but today we drain the squares on paper towels.

Serves 8 to 10　　　　　　　　　**—DREW OGLE,** *Christopher Place Resort, Newport*

This recipe was given to my grandfather by a friend, a country inn owner from Alabama, some twenty years ago.

—DREW OGLE

SPICED PEACHES

2 1-pound, 13-ounce cans peaches, halved or sliced

1⅓ cups sugar

1 cup apple cider vinegar

4 3-inch cinnamon sticks

2 teaspoons whole cloves

Drain syrup from peaches into a large saucepan; set peaches aside. Add sugar, vinegar, cinnamon and cloves to syrup (the cinnamon and cloves may be placed in a spice bag or tea ball). Bring to a boil over medium-high heat, stirring occasionally. Lower heat and simmer 10 minutes.

Stir peaches into syrup and simmer for 30 minutes to allow flavors to permeate the fruit. Remove spices and pour peaches and syrup into jars. Place lids on jars and refrigerate. May be served hot or chilled.

Fills approximately 3 pint jars　　　　**—ELIZABETH ANN JOHNSON,** *Athens*

My great-aunt used to make this recipe with fresh peaches, which was a lot of work. Now I make Spiced Peaches at Christmas for the family and also to give to friends as gifts.

—ELIZABETH ANN JOHNSON

TENNESSEE EGGNOG

12 eggs, separated

1 cup sugar

1 quart Jack Daniel's Black Label

¼ cup dark rum

1 quart half & half

1 quart heavy cream

In a large bowl, add the sugar to the egg yolks and beat until the mixture is light and smooth, or until you no longer feel the sugar particles.

Add the Jack Daniel's a little at a time, beating vigorously. Add rum and beat. Add coffee cream and beat. Whip heavy cream until soft peaks and fold in. Beat egg whites until stiff and fold in. Cover and let the eggnog stand for 2 days in the refrigerator to absorb flavors.

Serve in crystal punch bowl with a sprinkling of nutmeg.

Serves 20　　　　　　　　　**—PHILA HACH,** *Hachland Hill Inn, Clarksville*

My father always insisted on having eggnog on Christmas Eve, but he never spiked it. That way the kids could join in the fun.

—LINDA WISE-TUCKER, *formerly of Miner Hill*

MUSHROOM CASSEROLE

½ cup butter, divided in half
3 8-ounce packages sliced mushrooms
1½ cups herb-seasoned stuffing mix

2 cups shredded, sharp cheddar cheese
½ cup milk

Preheat oven to 325°F.

Over medium heat, melt ¼ cup butter in large skillet. Add mushrooms and cook until tender. Stir in stuffing mix straight from the box.

Spoon half the mushroom mixture into an 8-inch square, greased baking dish and sprinkle with 1 cup cheese. Add the rest of the mushroom mixture and the other cup of cheese. Dot with remaining ¼ cup butter and pour milk over casserole.

Bake for 30 minutes, until bubbling and cheese is melted.

Serves 8 to 10

—**YVONNE MINGLE,** *Murfreesboro*

This casserole is delicious with all meats, especially ham.

—**YVONNE MINGLE**

Formal dining room with crystal candolier, Rattle & Snap Plantation, Mount Pleasant

GRITS AND SMOKED OYSTER CASSEROLE

12 cups water
4 cups hominy grits (not instant)
1 cup butter (2 sticks), plus 2 tablespoons
2 tablespoons salt
½ teaspoon cayenne pepper
1 pound red peppers, diced
2 bunches green onions, sliced on bias
2 pounds smoked, shucked oysters
1 cup Monterey Jack cheese, grated
  (or Parmesan)
10 eggs
2 tablespoons chopped parsley

Preheat oven to 350°F.

In a large pot, combine water, grits, 1 cup butter, salt and cayenne and simmer over low heat until thick. Remove from heat.

In a sauté pan, sauté peppers and onions in 2 tablespoons butter until translucent. Add to cooked grits. Add oysters, cheese, eggs and parsley to grits and mix well.

Pour mixture into two 9 x 13-inch pans. Bake until set, approximately 30 minutes.

Makes 20 to 24 servings

—**CHEF JOHN FLEER,**
The Inn at Blackberry Farm, Walland

EGG CHEESE CASSEROLE

4 to 6 slices white sandwich bread, trimmed

1 medium onion, chopped

1 cup sliced fresh mushrooms

1 tablespoon butter

1 cup shredded cheddar cheese

1 cup shredded Swiss cheese

1 tablespoon flour

1¼ cups milk

4 large eggs, well beaten

1 tablespoon Dijon mustard

½ teaspoon garlic salt

Place bread slices in bottom of lightly buttered, 8-inch square casserole. Sauté onions and mushrooms in butter until soft. Spoon evenly over bread.

In a mixing bowl, combine cheese and flour; sprinkle evenly over bread. In another bowl, combine milk, eggs, mustard and garlic salt. Pour milk mixture over cheese. Cover and refrigerate overnight.

Remove from refrigerator and let stand at room temperature for 30 to 45 minutes. Preheat over to 375°F. Bake for 35 to 40 minutes, or until set. Let stand for 10 minutes before serving.

Sometimes I add cooked, crumbled bacon before the cheese, and other times I cook the bacon separately and serve it on the side.

Serves 6 to 8   **—ANNE CALDWELL RAMSEY,** *Lookout Mountain*

On Christmas morning, after everyone is up, I put the Egg Cheese Casserole in to bake so it will be ready when we are finished opening gifts. I serve the casserole with homemade cinnamon rolls and fresh orange slices—a menu that has just sort of evolved over the years. Some of the work is done ahead of time and the rest while we are all visiting in the kitchen.

—ANNE CALDWELL RAMSEY

On Christmas morning, we eat country ham, homemade biscuits, gravy, bacon, sausage, and coffee.

—JOHNNA R. ROGERS,
Union City

Christmas morning we serve a hearty mountain breakfast— biscuits, gravy, Belgian waffles with fresh fruit, two or three egg dishes, sausage, bacon, and ham.

—DREW OGLE,
Christopher Place Inn, Newport

Museum of Appalachia, Norris

Christmas in the Smokies
THE MUSEUM OF APPALACHIA

A fire blazes in an open hearth. Hot, spiced cider warming in a cast-iron pot emits the delicious aroma of Christmas. A couple of high-backed rocking chairs are placed in front of the fire. In one corner is a rope bed, covered with worn but brightly stitched patchwork quilts. There is a wooden cradle, a table with bench, and, off to the side, a steep set of stairs that lead to a tiny room upstairs. A family of eleven once lived in this cabin. Now restored, it is one of the many old-time cabins that are part of the Museum of Appalachia. This day, a fiddler and a banjo player play songs of the mountains. Evergreens adorn the simple mantle. It is a celebration of the Christmas season in Appalachia.

Founder and director of the Museum of Appalachia, John Rice Irwin grew up in East Tennessee, one of the many direct descendants of the pioneers who settled the Big Valley in the 1700s. As a young boy, John loved to listen to his grandparents, especially Grandfather Rice, talk about their ancestors. Over the years, Grandfather Rice gave John items that had been in the family for generations, saying that he "ought to start a little museum of these old-timey things."

While working as a school superintendent, John started accumulating examples of mountain life. Always a collector, he gathered tools, toys, crafts, and household items that represented a way of life he believed to be fast disappearing. His mission was confirmed at an auction when he saw a couple from out of state snap up an old cheddar churn to make into a lamp.

One Christmas tradition in our family (unless it was the Sabbath) was for all the men and boys to go rabbit hunting on Christmas after the noon meal, not so much to hunt rabbits as to spend some time together.

—JOHN RICE IRWIN, *Norris*

As John traveled throughout Southern Appalachia, his deep admiration for the mountain people grew as he gained their trust. He discovered them to be kind, gentle, and compassionate as well as resourceful and tough.

"I started the museum because some of the greatest people in the world lived and died in these mountains," says John. "Harry Truman's, Abraham Lincoln's, Mark Twain's, and Sam Rayburn's people were all from these parts. Those names will be remembered, but what about their mothers and fathers, who probably were just as ingenious, intelligent, and resourceful."

John knew his work was vitally important when he once asked a group of young girls who their grandmothers were. "I was astounded that most of them didn't know their grandmothers' maiden names," he said. "I reminded them that in twenty-five or thirty years their grandchildren might not remember their names."

Perhaps the most poignant feature of the museum is the Hall of Fame. Yes, there are mementos of famous people, but there are also pictures, letters, and belongings of people little known outside of their own mountain coves. Nevertheless, they are included in the Hall of Fame. One of the exhibits shows simply a list of names—eleven children, all in the same family, who died between the ages of two months and two years. "I want people to see this list of names and think how devastating it would be for a parent to lose just one child, let alone eleven."

Granny Toothman spinning wool

John founded the museum in 1962. He now runs it with the support of his wife, Elizabeth, the help of his daughter, Elaine, and a staff of forty. The Museum of Appalachia, which is also a working farm, is set in a picturesque valley just sixteen miles north of Knoxville in the town of Norris. Marked with handwritten signs, hundreds of thousands of old-time Appalachian items, from spinning wheels to handmade dulcimers, are displayed in the museum's main buildings. Over the years John has moved thirty-six buildings, most of them log structures, onto the museum grounds, where they are open to the public for self-guided tours. "Here people can see what it was like for nine or ten people to live comfortably in a one-room cabin," says John. "They knew how to respect each other."

The mountain people of Southern Appalachia were never ostentatious, and neither were their Christmas celebrations. In one old diary, Christmas wasn't mentioned at all, although it does note that one December 25 was a calving day. Many mountain people saw the Christmas holiday as simply a good time to get together. John remembers large numbers of his kin sitting together at Christmas, mostly just talking.

"My Uncle Lee was a great fiddler and we enjoyed music at other times of the year, but at Christmas people just wanted to talk, usually the men in one group and the women in another," he says. "You have to remember that mountain life was very isolated, especially back in the 1800s. People were hungry for news about other people and places."

Christmas tree in a pioneer cabin

Several of the museum's buildings are decorated with greenery at Christmastime. And a little cedar tree in the schoolhouse has paper chains and other handmade ornaments. But in general, the emphasis is on the congenial local musicians who play during the holidays, chatting with the visitors between songs. The museum also sells handcrafted gifts—gifts that may well be passed on to younger generations as a reminder of a way of life that once existed in the mountains of Southern Appalachia.

THE PLAY WAGON

by John Rice Irwin, Founder and Director, Museum of Appalachia

So many people I've met who have had interesting careers or have excelled at various endeavors almost always start talking about experiences they had with their grandfathers. My friend Alex Haley always said there was a special bond between grandparents and grandchildren because they had people in common against whom they could conspire. I had that special bond with all my grandparents.

Grandpa Rice was kind, warm, friendly, and humble but at the same time tough. He had worked in the coal mines as a kid, threshed wheat on the Cimmaron River in Oklahoma, and fought in the Spanish–American War. He was imbued with the strongest work ethic I've ever seen. He enjoyed what he was doing, but he never worked solely for the purpose of making money. My memories of him are so strong they almost exceed the time I spent with him.

As a kid I would spend an occasional weekend with Granny and Grandpa Rice. They lived on Bull Run Creek, a few miles north of Knoxville on what I thought was the most beautiful and enchanting old homestead imaginable. One time, when I was about five years of age, I spent much of the day stacking the aromatic oak and hickory logs that Grandpa split for the fireplace and Granny's cookstove—a big chore.

It was one of those cold, wintry days when the temperature dropped steadily as the day wore on and it soon began to snow. Finally, in the middle of the afternoon, Grandpa said it was getting too cold to work outside and that we'd better go in the house by the fire. Grandpa carried a big load of logs as we retired to the two-story house. The stack was so large it nearly covered his face, but he had added two special round logs on top, and I noticed that he also took his saw and some other tools. While we were sitting by the fire, he suddenly said, "We'll make you a little wagon."

He made the wagon based on the big farm wagons that I later learned were typically used throughout Appalachia. He had the rocking-bolster, the lynch pin, the coupling pole, and all these things. I knew how a wagon was supposed to be made and I was real pleased with it. He let me believe that I helped him make it. He was always wanting to make useful things, so he made this wagon for me to take corn to the chickens and haul wood to the house.

I played with the wagon in the barn most of the time. I remember one Christmas when it was so cold outside that I brought it in the house to play. Many years later, when the Fox Fire folks were looking to take pictures of handmade toys, Mother remembered that the play wagon had been relegated to the smokehouse. I brought it out and repaired it. It now it has a place of honor in the Museum of Appalachia.

It was tradition for Santa to deliver our presents either gift wrapped or in brown paper bags. I preferred the brown paper bags because I could always see the smudges of ash and soot where his hands had touched the inside of our chimney.

—LINDA WISE-TUCKER,
formerly of Miner Hill

As young children we always went to our grandparents at Christmas. We stayed in the parlor until we heard Santa's sleigh bells, then we could go in the big room where the tree and gifts were. Afterwards we went to a candlelight Christmas church service.

—LOIS BROWN MURPHY,
Maryville

John Rice Irwin's play wagon and Mack the doll

*My fondest memories of Christmas
start back in 1959. My husband
and I had purchased the house next
door to my mother and father-
in-law, and we would take our
children—at that time, three boys
—over to their house on Christmas
Eve. The whole family would
gather around my mother and
father-in-law and watch as they
opened their gifts. Afterwards,
we would sit at the kitchen table
until late in the evening and talk
while the younger children watched
the sky for Santa Claus. The gifts
that our in-laws opened were
never the most expensive and
their home was far from splendid,
but the love, laughter, and special
memories that we have as a family
will always be remembered and
cherished in each of our hearts.*

—**SHIRLIE H. BOLING,**
Rockford

Elves decorating a Christmas tree, The Inn at Blackberry Farm, Walland

*Even though my husband and I are
in our sixties, he still insists that
gifts are only opened on Christmas
morning. There are no exceptions,
not even for the grandchildren.*

—**HELEN NORMAND,**
Oak Ridge

ALICE GIBSON'S CHRISTMAS BASKET

*J*ohn Rice Irwin, founder and director of the Museum of Appalachia in Norris, Tennessee, has spent many years collecting items for the museum. Below is an account of his meeting with Alice Gibson, a mountain woman he encountered on one of his trips.

Alice and I had worked our way through her little mountain log cabin, finding interesting items here and there amid the myriad stacks of boxes, clothing, tools, and literally thousands of miscellaneous items, including several guns. Alice, who lives near the community of Norma in Scott County, Tennessee, was willing to sell many of the items, but when I opened the curtains to a small closet near the fireplace and brought out the pretty little white oak gizzard basket, she apologetically informed me that it wasn't for sale.

> Lord, Honey, that old basket belonged to my sister and I jest wouldn't sell it. I'll never forget she packed her Christmas dinner in that little basket and walked all the way from Caryville—hit took her all day. [It takes about 45 minutes in an automobile to drive this distance over some of the most rugged terrain in East Tennessee.] Rather than pack the basket back the next day, after she spent Christmas night with us, she give it to Mommie. And she took bad sick on her way back to Caryville and they had to take her out on a push car [on the railroad]. That was in 1928 and she took pneumonia and never did get over it. She died the 9th of March in 1929. So you can see why I wouldn't sell the little basket.

> I don't know how old it is, but hit wasn't new by no means when my sister brought it here. I jest think that Uncle John Overton may have made it. He was an old-time basketmaker. He lived over at Deane [near Norma]. It held three dozen eggs and we would keep our eggs in it 'til we got enough for a settin' and then we'd set a hen. And we used it to carry eggs to the store. We used it 'til the last few years and since then I've jest kept it as a sort of a keepsake.

Excerpted from BASKETS AND BASKET MAKERS IN SOUTHERN APPALACHIA *by John Rice Irwin. Reprinted with permission.*

Santa Claus sneaks into the inn's library late on Christmas Eve to stuff stockings for all our guests. They receive items from the area, such as homemade jellies or apple butter, or handmade rag dolls.

—DREW OGLE, *Christopher Place Inn, Newport*

My youngest brother has a big house and he puts gifts for about seventy-five people under the tree. It takes three hours just to hand them all out!

—AL SMITH, *Hixson*

We spend all night putting together the kids' toys to be ready for Christmas morning..

—JOHNNA R. ROGERS, *Union City*

Alex Haley owned the farm just across the street. He was often out of town at Christmas, but the thing about Alex was that he kept the spirit of Christmas all year round. There was never a man more generous. He traveled extensively and brought or sent back gifts for his friends from all over.

—JOHN RICE IRWIN, *Norris*

Old Cedar

Tucked away among a room of toys in the Museum of Appalachia is "Old Cedar," a rather plain, rough cedar rocking horse with a scruffy tail. But no rocking horse was ever more dear to a little boy. In 1922, when Luther Pyles was four years old, he showed his grandfather a picture of a rocking horse he had seen in a catalog. The next day his grandfather went to the woods, cut down a cedar tree, and made Old Cedar for Luther.

When Luther himself was in his eighties, he fondly recalled playing with Old Cedar. "I thought that was the greatest thing that ever was. They'd let me bring him in the house around Christmas, but most of the time I'd keep him in the barn. I rode that old horse all over Anderson County."

"Old Cedar," a hand-carved wooden play horse

Right after Christmas finishes one year, I make my list for the next year and take it to the post office to mail to Santa.

—**Carter Hach,** *(age 4) Nashville*

Every year I give a birthday gift to Jesus. The recipients vary—missionaries on furlough living in my area, my pastor and his family, friends having a hard year. I send them a check or cash explaining it is not from me to them, but that it is my birthday gift to Jesus. The letter explains that for that reason they may not thank me for it and may not even mention to me or to anyone else that they have received it. They may only speak of it to the Lord. The gift also comes with stringent rules that it may not be tithed, shared, put in the mission's offering, given away, or used in any other "spiritual" way. It is intended only for their pleasure.

—**Anonymous**

 We travel to visit with grandparents, aunts, and uncles before Christmas, and then spend Christmas Day at home with our three young children. Before opening presents from Santa, everyone curls up on Mommy and Daddy's bed to hear the Christmas story from the Bible. Although the kids are anxious to see what Santa left them, they get to hear what Christmas is all about, so they will remember and understand it when they are older.

—**Sarah Yann,** *Hermitage*

Christmas tree with antique toys, Franklin

Every gift I give at Christmas has to have a personal touch. For example, I always give my neighbor something to do with cats, such as a cat calendar, since she loves cats so much.

—**AL SMITH,** *Hixson*

I have a good Jewish friend who grew up with me. When we were kids she loved to come over to my house to help put the tinsel and decorations on the tree. She is now an artist, and to this day she still sends me a beautifully, artistically wrapped gift every Christmas.

—**MARY ALICE MASTELLONE,** *Memphis*

My step-grandfather was Spanish and his name was Angel, which as children we thought was great for Christmas. We would drive around and look at the lights and decorations near his home, especially a Model T Ford on an island in the middle of a lake with a Santa sitting in it, waving. When we got back from driving around, Santa Claus had already come!

—**LINDA TIPTON LAMB,** *Maryville*

On Christmas Eve each of our children is allowed to open one gift; the rest are opened Christmas morning.

—**KATHY TORGERSON,** *Gray*

I have a battery-operated Christmas pig that "oinks" Jingle Bells. I love to tease the kids with it, and they love to come in just to hear the pig.

—**DAN BROWN,**
Leonard's Barbecue, Memphis

Mantle with jolly Santas, Memphis

The Kingsport Santa Train

Every year on the Friday before Thanksgiving, you can feel the excitement in the air at the Kingsport railway station. Santa is coming! When the jolly old man arrives, he boards the CSX train, waving to all who have come to see him. Along with numerous community leaders, Santa rides the train up to Kentucky. But this is no ordinary train trip. Like any Santa vehicle, this one is filled with holiday gifts, food, and clothing for children (all donated by local merchants). In the true spirit of Christmas, Santa and his helpers deliver the gifts as the train makes stops throughout the Appalachian Mountains on its return trip to Kingsport the next day. The train arrives back in town just in time for Santa to join the annual Christmas parade.

The Santa Train arrives in Kingsport

MEMORIES OF A 1950s CHRISTMAS
by Judy Yost Jensen, formerly of Greenville

I grew up in a small town in East Tennessee in the 1950s. My daddy was a dentist and was often paid for his work with two pounds of fresh butter or two dozen eggs delivered once a week until the debt was paid. On Christmas Eve we would go to my granny's house across town. She always baked a hen with cornbread and sage stuffing and made scalloped oysters—crisp on the top with succulent oysters all the way from the Chesapeake Bay tucked inside.

After dinner, when the table was cleared and the tablecloth brushed for crumbs, all the gifts would be piled on the table and we would take turns opening them. My granddaddy, who was a telegraph operator for the Southern Railroad for fifty-seven years, would get enough cigars for the whole year. They came in those great boxes that kids turned into closets for doll clothes or hiding places for treasures. Most of the gifts were handmade by my granny, who had the handicraft skills of her generation. She made beautiful tatted flower bouquets on note cards, doll dresses with handmade bonnets and baskets to match, afghans, aprons, and pillow cases trimmed with delicate crochet.

But one of the best gifts was her homemade nut bread made with black walnuts picked out of those thick-hulled shells. You may think, "What a strange gift for a child," but East Tennessee was a modest place and you only had to taste a piece of this bread toasted with a light spread of butter to know why to this day I hunt high and low every year for some black walnuts to make Granny's nut bread for Christmas.

GRANNY'S BLACK WALNUT BREAD

4 cups flour
1 cup sugar
2 teaspoons baking powder
1 teaspoon salt
1¼ cups milk
1 egg, beaten
1½ cups black walnuts, chopped

Preheat oven to 350°F.

In a large bowl, combine flour, sugar, baking powder and salt. In a separate bowl, mix together milk and egg. Add the milk mixture to the flour and mix well. Stir in the nuts; batter will be dry and stiff.

Pour into a greased loaf pan and let stand 20 minutes. Bake for 45 minutes, or until toothpick comes out clean. Makes 1 loaf.

A TRIP TO JUNGLETOWN
by Dick Poplin, Shelbyville

Jungletown was really a place in Bedford County....We lived just a half a mile south of the store where the Jungletown road comes into the Midland-Rover Road, and from the little rise in the road near the store our barn could be seen....

Dad wasn't in the habit of sitting around the store as some did. We usually only went to the store to take eggs or chickens to sell and to buy the needed staples, sugar, salt, flour... coal oil for the lamps, and such other items which were kept by country stores that we needed from time to time.

I was still pretty young, but old enough to notice that on Christmas Eve, Dad would say along about bedtime, "Well, I think I'll walk up to Jungletown for a little while," and he wouldn't return until after we had gone to bed. The next morning the shoe boxes my brother and I had set out the night before would have apples, oranges, raisins on the stem (cluster raisins), sticks of candy, and perhaps a box of sparklers, and some English walnuts.

The year came when I was able to make association between Dad's trip to Jungletown and the box of goodies the next morning. That December 24 Dad continued to sit around the fire at home until I became uneasy, and I finally blurted out, "Hadn't you better go to Jungletown?"

Well, he did, and the next morning the expected fruit and candy were in the box. We didn't "hang stockings by the hearth with care." A box was simpler and held more.

I don't suppose things had changed much since Dad was a boy forty years earlier. His mother was left a widow with seven children, of which he was the youngest. He would set out his boots on Christmas Eve for the expected treats. One year he set them out again the next night, and either his mother or one of his sisters or brothers put an apple and an orange in them. With that success, he tried for the third time, but the next morning the boots had switches in them instead of fruit. He got the message and didn't try it anymore.

—Reprinted with permission from A YARD OF POPLIN by Dick Poplin, Bell Buckle Press, 1991.

My sister and I almost burst every Christmas morning waiting for the doors to open—our sign that we could run in and begin opening gifts

—CATHERINE CLARK, *Franklin*

My sister and I always made our own Christmas cards, tracing pictures from magazines and old Christmas cards, and then painting them with water colors. We also made Christmas gifts by painting black silhouettes on the inside of the glass in a picture frame.

—NANCY WAGGENER KING, *formerly of Nashville*

Christmas parade near Fort Louden

Christmas Roses

by Ramona Jones

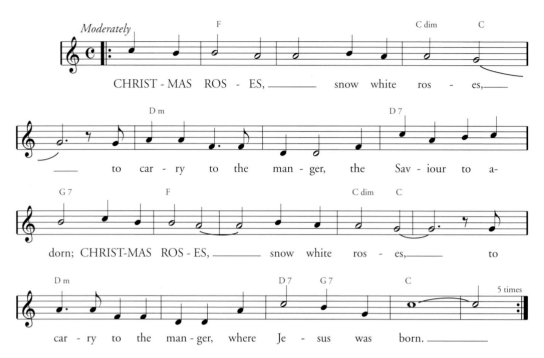

Moderately

CHRIST - MAS ROS - ES, _____ snow white ros - es, _____

_____ to car - ry to the man - ger, the Sav - iour to a-

dorn; CHRIST-MAS ROS - ES, _____ snow white ros - es, _____ to

car - ry to the man - ger, where Je - sus was born. _____

5 times

Once a little peasant girl
Was tending all her sheep
In fields so near to Bethlehem
Where Baby Jesus sleeps.
One early morn she saw three Kings
Ride by with gifts so rare.
She wished she too, could have a gift
To take to Jesus there!

Her tears were falling to the ground
As she told the Kings goodbye.
No gift to carry Jesus?
She could not help but cry,
But every little tear that fell
The Angels must have found
For as she turned to walk away,
There were roses all around!
(sing *Chorus*)

Chorus
CHRIST-MAS ROS-ES,
snow white ros-es,
to car-ry to the man-ger,
the Sav-iour to a-dorn;
CHRIST-MAS ROS-ES,
snow white ros-es,
to car-ry to the man-ger,
where Je-sus was born.

The Tipton place, Cades Cove

Beloved country music legend Grandpa Jones spent his last earthly Christmas in Tennessee in 1997. We remember with great fondness the many times he entertained us and made us laugh out loud. He will be missed.

The Friendly Beasts

Jesus our bro-ther, strong and good, Was hum-bly born in a sta-ble rude. And the

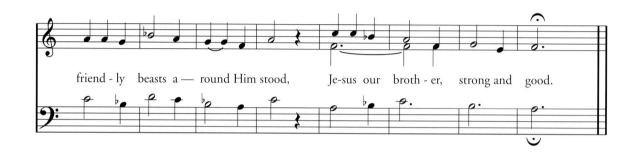

friend-ly beasts a — round Him stood, Je-sus our broth-er, strong and good.

Sheep grazing in front of a rare cantilevered barn,
Museum of Appalachia, Norris

"I," said the donkey, shaggy and brown,
"I carried His mother up the hill and down;
"I carried her safely to Bethlehem town,
"I," said the donkey, shaggy and brown.

"I," said the cow, all white and red,
"I gave Him my manger for His bed;
"I gave Him my hay to pillow His head,
"I," said the cow, all white and red.

"I," said the sheep with curly horn,
"I gave Him my wool for His blanket warm;
"He wore my coat on Christmas morn,
"I," said the sheep with curly horn.

"I," said the dove from rafters high,
"I cooed Him to sleep so He would not cry;
"We cooed Him to sleep, my mate and I,
"I," said the dove from the rafters high.

And every beast, by some good spell,
In the stable dark was glad to tell,
Of the gift he gave Emmanuel,
The gift he gave Emmanuel.

Overleaf: Winter reflection on the Cumberland Plateau
Opposite: Holy Family with the Three Wise Men, St. Luke's Episcopal Church, Memphis

One of our family traditions is reading the Christmas story from the Bible on Christmas Eve. Ever since our children were small, we have gathered in the living room, lit only by candles and the Christmas tree. As children grew old enough to read, they took a part, sometimes reading from their very own, brand-new Bible. This tradition has now been passed to the next generation, and this year we had three grandchildren join the five adults in the reading. As we handed an electric candle from person to person as they read, the younger ones sat there with eyes round with wonder, taking it all in. After the reading we say a prayer. It is a time for each of us to be still, to be thankful for our family, and to think of God's gift to us.

—**ROGER AND PHYLLIS THOMAS,** *Signal Mountain*

Gravel Hill Baptist Church, near Johnson City

Seventh-Day Adventist Church, Maryville

The Sunday before Christmas we would all go and decorate the church with greenery and lights. We climbed tall ladders and put candles in the windows. After midnight mass, we would have homemade pastries with hot chocolate.

—**MARY ALICE MASTELLONE,** *Memphis*

We like to read the Bible story to remember the true meaning of Christmas.

—**JOHNNA R. ROGERS,** *Union City*

I don't remember ever believing in Santa Claus, because to us Christmas celebrated the birth of the Christ Child.

—**NANCY WAGGENER KING,**
formerly of Nashville

Jesus' birthday—that's my thing about Christmas. I sing Happy Birthday to Him. I also lost my first tooth on Christmas Eve.

—**JOSEPH HACH,**
(age 6), Nashville

French Broad River Baptist Church

Our most important Christmas tradition is family communion. Because our family travels in evangelism, we have our own communion set, and we take the bread and juice together before we open our gifts. Communion involves prayer, praise, and gratitude. Each family member expresses thanks.

—**DR. BETTE STALNECKER,**
The Paschal House, Ripley

After Christmas dinner our entire family gathers together and I always read the story of Christ's birth from Luke 2.

—**MRS. JOHN L. ROSE,**
Signal Mountain

*Sulphur Springs
United Methodist Church*

We have a live Nativity scene in our church sanctuary. There always seems to be so many babies in the church that they have no trouble filling the spot of baby Jesus.

—**MICHAEL AND RAMONA FREDMAN,** *Memphis*

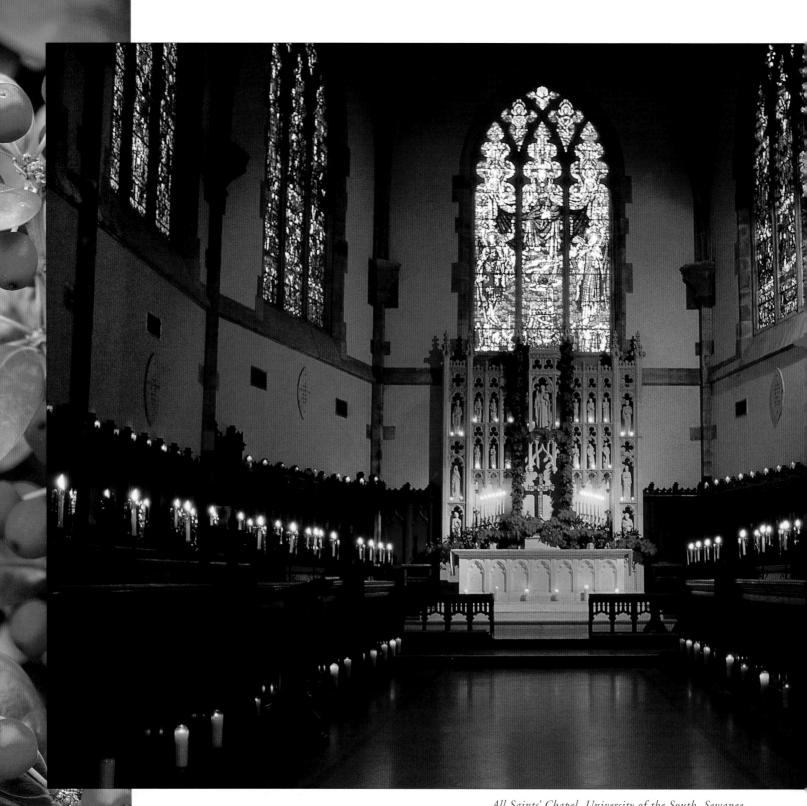

All Saints' Chapel, University of the South, Sewanee

 In December our church has an Alpine Christmas Village
in the gym. You walk into the village and there is a clock
shop, a candy shop, a gingerbread shop, and a church.
The kids go from place to place and pick up goodies with
Christmas scriptures attached to them. Nearly 900 children
came through last year.

—MICHAEL AND RAMONA FREDMAN, *Memphis*

Festival of Lessons and Carols

THE UNIVERSITY OF THE SOUTH

High on a mountaintop in Middle Tennessee, from the Gothic stone walls and stained glass windows of All Saints' Chapel, come the inspiring strains of the music of Christmas. For nearly forty years Tennessee residents have filled the chapel's pews in anticipation of hearing the annual Festival of Lessons and Carols at the University of the South in Sewanee.

It would be easy to imagine that one was listening to the choirs of Oxford or Cambridge, as All Saints' Chapel was designed to reflect the architecture of these famed English churches. Built of native sandstone, the chapel bears such a strong resemblance it is easy to forget that this is Tennessee. As Christmas approaches, the students, faculty, staff, and friends of the university decorate the chapel with greens from surroundings forests, replicating the simple style of English churches during the holiday season.

The annual festival services are so popular that worshipers must arrive early to get a seat. The scriptural text of the Christmas story is interwoven with both traditional and contemporary carols, utilizing the lovely voices of the University Choir, with the congregation occasionally joining in. Following the theme of darkness moving into light, the stirring age-old story of the birth of Christ unfolds on this beautiful Tennessee mountaintop.

Above: Preparation for the Festival of Lessons and Carols

Left: Choir by candlelight, prior to the processional into the darkened chapel

A People Apart

TENNESSEE'S AMISH COMMUNITY

For the Amish people of Tennessee, the meaning and the spirit of Christmas is observed throughout the year. December 25 is a time for quiet observance of the birth of Jesus, not an elaborate holiday.

The Amish are deeply spiritual men and women who live devoutly and peaceably, raising their families in the long and honorable traditions of their faith. These traditions include a simple lifestyle apart from a world where modern conveniences are commonplace—conveniences such as telephones, electricity, and even automobiles. Honest hard work, strong family ties, and worship make up the days of their lives. One would never find a decorated Christmas tree in an Amish home, or evidence that Santa Claus had visited. The Amish celebrate Christmas as they do everything else—in their own way.

There are both "old" and "new" Amish, and this often determines how they observe Christmas. In old Amish families, they gather at someone's home on Christmas Day to hear a sermon based on the birth of Jesus from the Gospel according to Luke. They sing German Christmas hymns (although the Amish speak both English and German, their services are still in German) and may perhaps share a meal. In general, there would be no gift giving, decorations, or holiday feast.

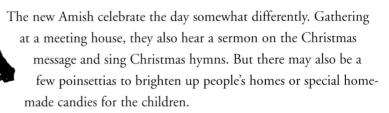

The new Amish celebrate the day somewhat differently. Gathering at a meeting house, they also hear a sermon on the Christmas message and sing Christmas hymns. But there may also be a few poinsettias to brighten up people's homes or special homemade candies for the children.

"Many families have not started the gift-giving tradition because it detracts from the spiritual significance of the season," says Mary Hosteller, who lives near Clarksville, just a few miles from the Tennessee border. "But I enjoy giving a few small gifts to the grandchildren."

Gifts are always practical, often religious books, educational games, or items of clothing. A young couple engaged to be married might present each other with a concordance to the Bible, says Mary, who runs a charming country store called "Grandma's Kitchen." Her suggestions for holiday desserts include jam cakes, coconut cakes, and—of course—boiled custard.

Peanut brittle has been a Christmas tradition in Fanny Miller's family for nearly forty years. Fanny and her daughter Edna, also members of the Amish community, are said to make the world's best peanut brittle, according to the many locals and tourists who have sampled it. For many years Fanny just made the delightful confection for candy sales at school, using peanuts grown on the family farm. But it became so popular that people wanted more, and the Millers starting giving candy to family and friends as holiday gifts.

According to Edna, one of the lovely traditions of the Amish young people at Christmas is to go caroling, often hayride-style in horse-drawn wagons. They visit widows, shut-ins, and others who might especially enjoy some cheerful Christmas music, this time sung in English.

All year long, the simplicity of Jesus' message is central to the Amish way of life. During the Christmas season, the devotion of these gentle people is evidenced further as they observe the real meaning of the day their own unique way.

Hanukkah

On a cold night in winter, as the last light of day fades across the cities and towns of Tennessee, the windows in many homes glow with the warmth of a brightly lit menorah. Known as the Festival of Lights, Hanukkah honors both the Jewish people's special covenant with God and a great historic event in their epic history.

In 165 B.C., Judah Maccabee, his brothers, and their small army defeated the powerful Syrian tyrant Antiochus. It was a miracle of great proportions, but a more significant miracle occurred when the Hebrew people went to reconsecrate their temple, which had been stripped of sacred items and desecrated with Syrian idols. All that could be found was one small cruse of holy oil, which was not nearly enough for the purification process. In faith, the people lit the oil and it miraculously lasted for eight days, long enough for new oil to be made.

Hanukkah commemorates this miracle, and the eight candles of the menorah represent the eight days that the oil burned. The lighting of the menorah is a special event in Jewish families. One candle is lit on the first night of Hanukkah, with another candle lit each of the following nights, until all are shining. There are actually nine candles on the menorah, with the extra used to light all the others. The dates of the festival vary from year to year, but it always starts at sunset on the 25th day of Kislev according to the Hebrew lunar calendar—which can be as early as November 28 or as late as December 24.

Joe and Freddi Felt of Memphis try to spend Hanukkah as a family whenever possible, gathering together their grown children and grandchildren. As with all Jewish holidays, Hanukkah is family celebration. Each season the Felts host a big party for family and friends, with a dinner menu that includes many traditional foods, such as Freddi's delicious homemade latkes—potato pancakes served with applesauce and sour cream.

While gift giving is kept to a minimum, children are given small presents on the first seven nights of Hanukkah and a larger present on the eighth night. Children play with the traditional dreidel, a simple spinning top with the Hebrew words "a miracle happened there" written on it. Depending on how the dreidel lands, the child spinning it either receives a small prize of gold-foil wrapped chocolate coins, or forfeits some he or she has already won. When her children were little, Freddi used to make a large dreidel-shaped centerpiece and fill it with candy and other goodies, so when children came over, they could reach in and pull out a surprise.

Hanukkah is a special time when the Jewish people thank God for their blessings and the miracles of the past. Each night before the menorah is lit, prayers are offered in both Hebrew and English.

THE HANUKKAH PRAYERS
To be said while lighting the candles of the menorah

OFFERED THE FIRST NIGHT:
Praise be Thou, Lord our God, King of the Universe who has kept us alive and has preserved us and enabled us to reach this season.

OFFERED EACH NIGHT:
Praise be Thou, Lord our God, King of the Universe who has sanctified us by His commandments and has commanded us to kindle the Hanukkah lights.

OFFERED EACH NIGHT:
Praise be Thou, Lord our God, King of the Universe who wrought miracles for our fathers in days of old at this season.

Hanukkah lights in December

Native American

Tennessee's history is filled with stories of Native Americans, mostly about the Cherokee, who have lived in the Great Smoky Mountains of North Carolina and Tennessee for hundreds of years. Today, many tribes are represented in Tennessee, as job opportunities in metropolitan areas and at military installations have drawn many people of Indian heritage to the state.

"You could call Tennessee a sort of melting pot of Indian culture," says Gary White Deer, director of the Tennessee Native American Indian Association in Nashville and himself a Choctaw. "In addition to Cherokee, I have met Chickasaws, Apaches, Ottawas, Pawnees, Seminoles, Northern Cheyennes, Oneidas, Osages, Tuscaroras, Navajos, Pueblos, and many others. They are enrolled in tribes that are recognized in other states, but they live and work in Tennessee." Near Memphis there is a group of Choctaw Indians who came nearly forty-five years ago as sharecroppers and settled on federal trust land—the closest thing to a reservation in Tennessee.

Celebrations vary from tribe to tribe and often have little in common, although many tribes gather for powwows—colorful get-togethers with dancing and singing. Most of the Indians who live in Tennessee have adopted other religious faiths, primarily Christianity, and they celebrate Christmas according to the traditions of their particular denomination. Sometimes Native American families will decorate a cedar tree for Christmas and burn it afterward as a traditional symbol of purification.

"It is easy for us as Indians to relate to the real feeling of Christmas," says Gary White Deer, "because the concepts of sharing and of the importance of family have always been very much a part of Indian culture. We worry, though, that the commercial side of the holidays is being adopted too readily by our children."

"When I was a boy," Gary continues, "there were families that refused to buy Christmas presents. The only gifts were those made with their own hands. We called it 'Indian Christmas.' It took away the feeling of obligation and became a true gift. I wouldn't mind seeing 'Indian Christmas' happen all over Tennessee."

FRIED CORN MEAL MUSH

1¼ cups corn meal
1 teaspoon salt
4 cups cold water
3 tablespoons butter

Mix together 1 cup corn meal and salt. Stir in 1 cup cold water.

In a saucepan, bring 3 cups of water to a boil. Gradually stir in meal mixture. Cook over low heat, stirring constantly, until thick (about 10 minutes). Pour into lightly greased loaf pan and place waxed paper over surface of batter. Refrigerate four hours or overnight.

Remove waxed paper and cut into about 12 slices. Melt butter in a frying pan. With remaining ¼ cup of corn meal, dip each slice in corn meal and fry in hot butter until both sides are brown and crisp. This is delicious served with syrup.

Makes about 12 slices

—RAMONA "MRS. GRANDPA" JONES
From the GRANDPA JONES FAMILY COOKBOOK

Kwanzaa

"Kwanzaa represents a return to values handed down in African-American families for many generations," says Vilma Fields of the African-American Cultural Center in Chattanooga. "It reminds us of our ancestors in Africa as they celebrated the first fruits of the harvest."

Meaning "first" in Swahili, Kwanzaa is a colorful festival that takes place December 26 through January 1. It is a time of feasting, singing, dancing, storytelling, arts and crafts, and prayer. Kwanzaa was founded in America more than thirty years ago to promote unity and a return to old-time values among African-Americans. Many of the festivities take place in community centers, although it is important, says Ms. Fields, that families teach their children the meaning of Kwanzaa as well. "We focus on the children, and get the teenagers to help us with our activities. It's a matter of passing along the heritage of previous generations."

All activities revolve around the lighting of the kinara, which holds seven candles representing the seven principles of Kwanzaa. As the candles are lit one day at a time, each principle is examined and explained. Oral traditions are central to Kwanzaa celebrations, although poetry and passages from books are also used for readings and dramatic presentations. Kwanzaa feasts are simple, including foods such as beans, rice, potato pies, chicken, collard greens, and fruit—much as their ancestors ate.

"I like to think that the spirituality of Kwanzaa draws attention away from the commercialism of Christmas," says Ms. Fields. "Kwanzaa is a time to value your family and get back to basics. By embracing our past, we make our future brighter."

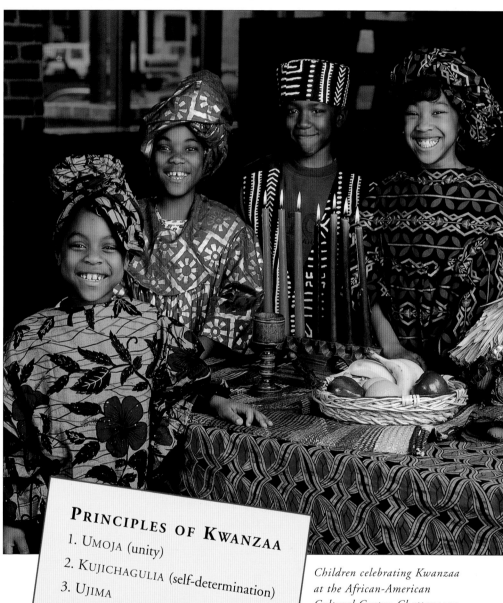

PRINCIPLES OF KWANZAA
1. UMOJA (unity)
2. KUJICHAGULIA (self-determination)
3. UJIMA
   (collective work and responsibility)
4. UJAMMA (cooperative economics)
5. NIA (purpose)
6. KUUMBA (creativity)
7. IMANI (faith)

Children celebrating Kwanzaa at the African-American Cultural Center, Chattanooga

The Inn at Blackberry Farm

Between Maryville and Townsend, just a few miles from a busy highway, there exists a whole other world. Here, tucked into the foothills of the Great Smoky Mountains, is a 1,000-acre getaway called The Inn at Blackberry Farm.

As visitors turn off the highway at a glistening white fence, they travel the few final miles through towering trees. High-back wooden rocking chairs, lined up on the verandah like a welcoming committee, invite guests to sit for a spell to enjoy one of the loveliest views in the state. Inside, the inn is the epitome of country comfort and elegant living— a kind of pampered luxury with a put-your-feet-up-and-stay-awhile feeling. "Rugged yet refined is how we describe ourselves," says Kreis Beall, who owns The Inn at Blackberry Farm with her husband Sandy.

This philosophy is also reflected in the inn's menu. Director and Executive Chef John Fleer is famous for his "foothills cuisine," which he describes as a combination of down-home country cooking and haute cuisine. His grandmother's cookbook is always handy for inspiration, but his style is his own unique creation, combining traditional ingredients in new and different ways. Chef Fleer, who was born on Christmas, admits to loving the holiday, and one of his seasonal favorites is Tennessee Chess Pie.

At Christmastime the inn is decorated both inside and out. Traditional wreaths made with greenery and big red bows are placed in every window. Natural garlands are strung throughout the inn, with boxwood garlands in the more formal rooms and pine and hemlock in the others. Of the inn's sixteen Christmas trees, the most elegant is in the living room, gracefully adorned with gold ornaments and dried pink and red roses—Kreis's favorite. The guests tend to favor the more fanciful "fly-fishing tree," complete with multicolored flies, miniature fishing poles, and a fly-fishing Santa. The "Christmas tree forest" consists of five live pines decorated only in tiny white lights. Their root balls are wrapped in colorful quilts because the trees will be planted on the grounds after the holidays. For the nostalgic, the tree in the dining room shimmers with big, old-fashioned colored lights and glass balls, with a beautiful collection of antique dolls sitting prettily around its base.

Guests at The Inn at Blackberry Farm design their own holiday activities, but one can be assured it is all done in style and comfort. Chef John Fleer always prepares one of his specialties—fried turkey, a Christmas tradition at The Inn at Blackberry Farm.

Top: The Inn at Blackberry Farm, Walland

Above: Banquet table in the dining room

Sunset and winter storm over Mount LeConte

FRIED TURKEY

12- to 15- pound turkey
1 ½ gallons peanut oil

Marinade
1 ½ cups olive oil
1 cup champagne vinegar
½ cup melted butter
¼ cup Worcestershire sauce
¼ cup chopped shallots
½ cup chopped basil
¼ cup water
1 tablespoon lemon juice

1 tablespoon Frank's Hot Sauce
1 teaspoon salt
1 teaspoon black pepper
¼ teaspoon cayenne pepper powder

Turkey Rub
2 tablespoons barbecue sauce
2 tablespoons chili powder
1 tablespoon cumin
1 tablespoon coriander
1 tablespoon lemon pepper
1 teaspoon black pepper

Remove gizzards and tie legs of turkey together with thin wire.

Combine all marinade ingredients and let stand for an hour. Strain through a fine-mesh strainer. Using a veterinary hypodermic needle, inject the marinade into all parts of the turkey.

Combine Turkey Rub ingredients and mix to form a smooth paste. Put some of the rub in the palms of your hands and rub onto meat, leaving no clumps. Wrap turkey tightly in plastic wrap and let sit overnight in refrigerator.

In a large stock pot, heat the peanut oil to 400°F. Tie a coat hanger to the wire leg tie of the turkey to use as a handle. Immerse turkey in oil so that it is completely covered. Using an accurate, high-temperature thermometer, keep oil at 350°F degrees. Cook the turkey for 35 to 40 minutes, until a dark golden brown.

Be very careful removing the turkey. Use a spatula or tongs to support the turkey as you remove it from the hot oil. Be sure to drain oil from turkey cavity. Let turkey sit for 15 minutes before carving.

Serves 15 to 20

—**CHEF JOHN FLEER,** *The Inn at Blackberry Farm, Walland*

Years ago we started a holiday tradition to have a Christmas program between the main course and dessert. The preparation of the program is as important as the preparation of the food. The program varies, but it may include scripture, songs (usually read rather than sung since my family is most unmusical), poems, stories, and various readings collected from books, magazines, tracts, Christmas letters, or even from something heard over the radio. The program is designed to focus on the true meaning of Christmas—that God became man to live and die for us so we can spend eternity with Him. Oftentimes everyone is given an opportunity to share something Christmassy. We may include choral or antiphonal readings. And we always have prayer.

—**JANE ELLEN HODGES,** *Dayton*

Barbecue is very big in Memphis and many people serve barbecue for their office Christmas parties. A lot of people barbecue on Christmas Day because their families from out of town want it instead of turkey. For former residents who can't get back for the holidays, families and friends will send our Memphis barbecue as a holiday gift.

—**LORETTA HOPPER,**
Leonard's Barbecue, Memphis

On Christmas afternoon we have a twenty-pound turkey with a herb and cornbread stuffing, sweet potato casserole, cranberry Jell-O salad topped with marshmallows, homemade cranberry sauce, broccoli casserole, wheat rolls, ambrosia, coconut cake, and pumpkin pies with whipped cream.

—**BONNIE ALLIN,** *Chattanooga*

My grandparents came from Italy, so it was the tradition in our house to have lots of food. At Christmas my mother would make about a hundred dozen raviolis. There were so many I never wanted to make them myself. But after Mother passed on, I realized that ten dozen or so was more my speed.

—**MARY ALICE MASTELLONE,**
Memphis

Traditional "foothills cuisine" Christmas dinner, The Inn at Blackberry Farm

ROAST TURKEY WITH GIBLET GRAVY

1 20-pound turkey, dressed	*Mirepoix*
Salt and pepper	2 onions, chopped
Oil	2 carrots, chopped
	2 stalks celery, chopped

On Christmas Eve we usually go to Ramona's mom's house and she makes a turkey dinner. Everyone gathers from near and far, so a big crowd converges on Mother. We have a family gift exchange there. Our children open gifts at home on Christmas morning.

—MICHAEL AND RAMONA FREDMAN, *Memphis*

Preheat oven to 325°F.

Remove giblets from cavity of turkey. Check inside of turkey to make sure it has been cleaned well. Lock the wings in place by twisting the wing tips behind the back of the turkey. Season the inside of the turkey with salt and pepper. Rub the skin thoroughly with oil.

Place turkey in a roasting pan and add the Mirepoix, placing the vegetables all around the turkey; you may also put some vegetables inside the turkey. To make the Mirepoix, finely dice the onions, carrots, and celery, and simmer together in two tablespoons of butter until lightly browned.

Put turkey in oven and baste with drippings every 30 minutes by spooning the fat in the pan over the turkey. Turkey is done when a thermometer inserted into the thickest part of the inside of the thigh reads 180°F. Total roasting time is about 5 hours.

While turkey is roasting, place the giblets (the heart, gizzard and neck) in a saucepan (reserve the liver for another use, such as adding it to a bread dressing). Cover the giblets with water and simmer over low heat until giblets are very tender, about 2 to 3 hours. Reserve both the giblets and the cooking broth for gravy.

Remove turkey from the roasting pan and let stand in a warm place at least 15 minutes before carving. Serve with Giblet Gravy.

—CHEF RICHARD GERST, *Opryland Hotel, Nashville*

CHRISTMAS NURSE
by Jane Ellen Hodges, Dayton

I am a nurse and usually have to work Christmas Day, so Betty, my sister, will often come to the hospital to have dinner with me. One year I was on duty in the Intensive Care Unit and had no one to relieve me, so Betty went to the cafeteria and brought two trays back to ICU. There we ate while I frequently jumped up to check on my patients.

Another year on Christmas Day, we met an older woman, Eleanor, who was at the hospital looking after a friend. Eleanor had lost the last of her family the year before, so Betty and I invited her to join us for Christmas dinner, which we ate right there in the hospital room. The following year I called Eleanor to invite her to join us again for Christmas dinner. "You mean in the hospital?" she asked. "No," I said, "not this time. I don't have to work this year." So Eleanor came to our house for Christmas Day.

GIBLET GRAVY

3 quarts chicken stock	Giblets and giblet broth
¾ cup bread flour	(see above recipe)
	Salt and pepper

Drain off and save the fat from the roasting pan. Set the pan with the Mirepoix and drippings on the range over low heat. Slowly reduce (cook down) the liquid as the Mirepoix browns.

Deglaze pan with 1 quart of chicken stock. Pour into a large saucepan with the rest of the chicken stock and the giblet broth. Bring to a simmer. Remove as much grease as possible.

Make a roux with flour and fat drained from the roasting pan. Beat the roux into the gravy to thicken it. Simmer at least 15 minutes, until the gravy is smooth and no raw-flour taste remains. Strain and season to taste with salt and pepper. Chop or dice the giblets very fine and add to the gravy.

—CHEF RICHARD GERST, *Opryland Hotel, Nashville*

HOLIDAY ALMOND BOURSON

1 8-ounce package fat-free cream cheese, softened

1 8-ounce package regular cream cheese, softened

2 bunches green onions, chopped

1 clove garlic, minced

1 6-ounce can roasted, salted almonds

Mix all ingredients thoroughly by hand; do not use an electric mixer or it becomes runny. On a platter, mold mixture into a pinecone-shaped figure, flat on the bottom and slightly rounded across the top. When looking down on it, it should look like a pinecone cut in half, cut-side down (see below). Line almonds in even rows across mound. Garnish with a sprig of pine needles and serve with crackers as an appetizer.

Serves approximately 20

—**CATHERINE CLARK,** *Franklin*

My mother served this every year before the neighborhood Santa parade on Christmas Eve. Friends from church, the office, and distant relatives came to celebrate. All the children anticipated what Santa would bring that night after the parade.

—**CATHERINE CLARK**

SWEET POTATOES

5 pounds sweet potatoes

¾ cup butter

1 cup light cream (or hot milk)

¼ cup brown sugar

1 teaspoon cinnamon

½ teaspoon nutmeg

4 to 6 ounces marshmallows

Peel and eye sweet potatoes and cut into uniform sizes. In a large pot, cover potatoes with water and simmer until tender. Drain well and let potatoes steam dry for a few minutes.

Pass the potatoes through a food miller or ricer into the bowl of a mixer. Beat in butter. Then beat in cream (or hot milk if you prefer), adding enough for a consistency that is soft and moist but firm enough to hold its shape.

Add the brown sugar, cinnamon and nutmeg. Whip briefly at high speed until potatoes are light and fluffy; do not overwhip. Place potatoes in casserole dish and top with marshmallows.

Preheat oven to 400°F. Cook potatoes, uncovered, for about 10 minutes, until marshmallows are golden brown (watch carefully so marshmallows don't burn).

Serves a large group

—**CHEF RICHARD GERST,** *Opryland Hotel, Nashville*

My younger daughter always creates an appetizer that we have while getting everything together for Christmas Eve.

—**ANNE RAMSEY,**
Lookout Mountain

In our growing-up years we always spent Christmas Day with Mother's brother, Uncle Ralph, and his family. But as we grew up and the children all married and had families of their own, that tradition fell by the wayside. So we would invite people who did not have families of their own to be with on Christmas. Mother had taught us that Christmas was to be celebrated and shared with others

—**JANE ELLEN HODGES,**
Dayton

Every Christmas Eve for years we have had homemade cream of potato soup for dinner. After dinner we often go caroling at a local nursing home.

—**KATHY TORGERSON,** *Gray*

Our family just likes to get together at Christmas. We don't do anything special, although we do have a traditional turkey with dressing, sweet potatoes, caramel cake, and a dish of fruit.

—**SALLY BUSH,** *Clarksville*

*Our traditional Christmas begins
with Christmas Eve dinner. We
grill a filet of beef and serve it
with a classic Bearnaise sauce. To
that we add twice-baked potatoes
and Spinach Artichoke Casserole.
I used to make homemade rolls,
but not since Sister Shubert's yeast
rolls came into our life. They are
wonderful!*

—ANNE CALDWELL RAMSEY

SPINACH ARTICHOKE CASSEROLE

1 large onion, chopped

1 teaspoon butter

2 10-ounce packages frozen chopped
  spinach, thawed and drained

1 8½-ounce can artichoke hearts,
  drained and chopped

1 8-ounce carton sour cream
  (low-fat or fat-free may be used)

Dash of Worcestershire sauce

Salt and pepper to taste

¾ cup freshly grated Parmesan cheese

Preheat oven to 350°F.

In a skillet, sauté onions in butter until clear. In a large bowl, combine spinach and
artichoke hearts, having drained off as much liquid as possible. Add onions and sour cream.
Season to taste with Worcestershire sauce and salt and pepper.

Place in lightly greased or sprayed 2-quart casserole and sprinkle with Parmesan cheese.
Bake for 25 minutes until bubbling and golden brown.

Serves 6 to 8   **—ANNE CALDWELL RAMSEY,** *Lookout Mountain*

*This is delicious with turkey and
mashed potatoes! Grandmother
Scott brought this dish to all our
holiday dinners. The grandchildren
were introduced to mushrooms at
a young age and they all love them.*

—PATTY HOLBROOK

GRANDMOTHER'S SHERRIED MUSHROOMS

2 pounds mushrooms

¼ cup butter (see note)

Scant ½ cup flour

¼ cup half-and-half (see note)

2 tablespoons dry sherry

Salt and pepper to taste

Trim stems and slice mushrooms; or you can leave them whole if you prefer. Melt
butter in a skillet and sauté mushrooms, seasoning with salt and pepper. Add flour by the
tablespoonful then the half-and-half by the same method. Add sherry and salt and pepper
to taste. Transfer to a small casserole and serve warm as a side dish; it reheats easily.

Note: Increasing the butter and half-and-half to ½ cup each makes a gravy-like consistency.

Makes 4 to 6 servings   **—PATTY HOLBROOK,** *Johnson City*

*Since we have turkey and ham with
all the trimmings at Thanksgiving,
our main Christmas meal is a
grilled steak with a potato casserole, salad, and dessert. It doesn't
take much time and we can enjoy
opening the presents and having
family fun.*

—ANNE AND WILLIAM ALLEN,
Chattanooga

HOLIDAY PEAS

1 medium onion, sliced

¼ cup butter

1 10-ounce can mushroom soup

1 4-ounce can sliced mushrooms

½ cup slivered almonds

½ cup water chestnuts

1 tablespoon Worcestershire sauce

Salt and pepper to taste

3 10-ounce packages frozen green peas

Preheat oven to 350°F.

In a large pan, sauté onion in butter until tender. Add remaining ingredients, except
peas, to sauté pan and stir. Gently fold in uncooked peas. Pour into a buttered, 9 x 13-inch
casserole, and bake for 30 minutes.

Makes 8 to 10 servings

—RAMONA "MRS. GRANDPA" JONES *From the* GRANDPA JONES FAMILY COOKBOOK

CHRISTMAS SALAD

1 ½ cups fresh cranberries
Crisp head of iceberg or Bibb lettuce
8 seedless oranges, peeled and sliced

2 medium Spanish onions, sliced thin
French salad dressing

Chop cranberries by hand or in a food processor. Tear lettuce and arrange on individual salad plates. Add oranges, onions and cranberries. Serve with French dressing.

Serves 8 to 10

—**PHILA HACH**, *Hachland Hills Inn, Clarksville*

CARROT RAISIN SALAD

2 cups shredded carrots
½ cup raisins
½ cup pecans
½ cup mini marshmallows

¼ cup honey
¼ cup pineapple juice
1 teaspoon lemon juice

Combine all ingredients and mix well. Chill at least one hour and serve. Enjoy!

Serves approximately 12

—**CHEF RICHARD GERST**, *Opryland Hotel, Nashville*

WECK'S BUTTER ROLLS

Rolls
1 cup butter
1 tablespoon sugar
2 eggs
¼ teaspoon salt
3 cups flour
1 package yeast dissolved in
¼ cup warm water (as warm as your finger can stand) with 1 tablespoon sugar

Paste
¾ cup finely chopped pecans
½ cup sugar
3 tablespoons heavy cream

Icing
1 cup powdered sugar
3 to 4 teaspoons warm milk or cream

In a mixing bowl, cream butter and sugar. Add eggs and salt, and beat well. Mix in flour and yeast mixture. Divide dough into 4 parts. Roll each part into a circle and then cut each circle into 6 wedges.

Combine paste ingredients and spread sparingly onto each wedge. Roll up wedges and curve into crescents. Place rolls on a greased cookie sheet and let rise for 1 ½ to 2 hours.

Preheat oven to 350°F. Bake rolls for 10 to 15 minutes until golden brown. Mix together icing ingredients, stirring until all lumps are broken up and dissolved. Drizzle icing over rolls while still warm.

Makes 24 rolls

—**HONEY RODGERS**, *Nashville*

Our traditional Christmas Eve dinner is Brie with cranberry salsa, cream of carrot soup, grilled salmon with dill sauce, garden salad, twice-baked potatoes, steamed broccoli, Parker House rolls, and various dessert bars and cookies.

—**PATTY AND JOHN HOLBROOK**, *Johnson City*

Every year we must have French Quarter Green Bean Casserole, a recipe that came from SOUTHERN LIVING magazine. One year we didn't serve it and everyone protested.

—**CARLA PARMELE**, *Knoxville*

Weck was a Swiss deaconess who befriended my Kentucky grandparents fifty-plus years ago. My mother made these at Christmas and we have traditionally given a tray to friends for Christmas morning.

—**HONEY RODGERS**

HACHLAND HILLS ROLLS

3½ cups flour
1 cup hot water
1 egg
⅓ cup sugar
¼ cup oil

1 teaspoon salt
1 package yeast
  (dissolved in ⅓ cup warm water)
Dash yellow food coloring, if desired

In a mixing bowl, combine all ingredients except for 1 cup flour and the yeast
mixture. Beat until smooth. Add yeast mixture and food coloring. Allow to rise 1 hour,
or until doubled in size.

Preheat oven to 350°F.

Turn out dough and knead until smooth on a lightly floured board, using the 1 cup
reserved flour. Roll dough out to ½-inch thickness and cut with small cutter. Place rolls on
a greased cookie sheet, and allow to rise again until doubled. Bake for 15 to 20 minutes, or
until golden brown. Turn out at once.

Sneckins
(This is a topping for Hachland Hill Rolls. This version is baked in an iron skillet.)

¾ cup butter   ¾ cup light brown sugar   ¾ cup chopped pecans

Dot the bottom of an iron skillet with butter. Cover butter with brown sugar, then
chopped pecans. Cover with rolls touching each other. As above, preheat oven to 350°F
and bake for 15 to 20 minutes, or until golden brown. Turn out at once.

Yields approximately 1 dozen rolls   **—PHILA HACH,** *Hachland Hills Inn, Clarksville*

TOPPING FOR FRESH FRUIT SALAD

⅓ cup pineapple juice
1½ tablespoons lemon juice
1 egg, lightly beaten
½ cup sugar

1 level teaspoon cornstarch
½ pint whipping cream
Dash of salt

Pour pineapple and lemon juice into the top of a double boiler. Add egg, sugar and
cornstarch. Cook over medium-high heat until thick, stirring continuously. Cool.

Beat cream until stiff. Fold into juice mixture. Add salt.

Tops 12 individual fruit salads   **—C. RITA GROSECLOSE,** *Kingsport*

STRAWBERRY JELL-O SALAD

1 3-ounce package cherry Jell-O
2 cups boiling water
1 20-ounce can crushed pineapple
1 10-ounce box frozen strawberries, thawed

1 3-ounce package cream cheese, softened
½ cup chopped pecans
½ cup sour cream (more if desired)

In a medium bowl, dissolve Jell-O in boiling water. Stir in pineapple and strawberries,
with juices. Pour half of mixture into a 2-quart mold and refrigerate until firm.

Mix together cream cheese, nuts and sour cream. Spread on top of congealed Jell-O.
Pour remaining Jell-O mixture into mold and refrigerate until firm. Can be served in the
mold or unmolded. To unmold, dip the pan in tepid water and turn out over a plate.

Serves 8   **—KATHIE GOTT,** *formerly of Hendersonville*

CRANBERRY CASSEROLE

Fruit Filling
3 cups diced apples
2 cups fresh cranberries
1 cup sugar
1 teaspoon cinnamon

Topping
1 ½ cups quick-cooking oats
½ cup light brown sugar
½ cup chopped pecans
⅓ cup flour
¼ cup milk

Preheat oven to 350°F.

Mix filling ingredients together and spread in a 13 x 9-inch baking dish. Mix topping ingredients and spread over fruit filling. Bake for 45 minutes until golden brown.

Serves 8 to 10

—YVONNE MINGLE, *Murfreesboro*

Our traditional meal has always been on Christmas Day and includes turkey with dressing (although sometimes a ham), sweet potatoes in orange halves, scalloped oysters, green beans, cranberry salad, hot rolls, and for dessert pumpkin and mincemeat pies.

—LOIS BROWN MURPHY,
Maryville

A friend shared this Cranberry Casserole recipe with me years ago. It is especially good with turkey dinners.

—YVONNE MINGLE

CRANBERRY BLACK WALNUT RELISH

½ cup brandy
½ cup orange juice
½ cup rice vinegar
½ cup minced red onion
½ tablespoon orange zest

½ teaspoon mustard seed
¼ teaspoon salt
2 cups sugar
24 ounces fresh cranberries (2 bags)
1 ¼ cups black walnuts, toasted

In a large saucepan, combine brandy, orange juice, vinegar, onion, orange zest, mustard seed and salt. Cook over medium heat, stirring occasionally, reduce until almost dry.

Add sugar and cranberries and cook on medium-low heat, stirring often, until most of the cranberries have popped.

Remove from heat and fold in black walnuts. Chill before serving.

Serves 10

—CHEF JOHN FLEER, *The Inn at Blackberry Farm, Walland*

On Christmas Eve we attend church as a family, and on the way home we drive around to look at all the Christmas lights. Then we have a special dinner, usually pork loin with cherry sauce, potato casserole, green beans, bread, and perhaps a congealed strawberry salad. We wake up early on Christmas morning and listen to my father read the story of Jesus' birth before we open gifts.

—REBECCA MILLER WEEKS,
Brentwood

Our Christmas dinner is celebrated on Christmas Eve. We have turkey and cornbread dressing, honey-baked ham, mashed potatoes, asparagus salad, green beans, pumpkin and mincemeat pies, apple stack cake, and assorted cookies.

—BONNIE ALLIN, *Chattanooga*

Poinsettias on the main staircase, Graceland, Memphis

Elvis' life-sized nativity scene

Christmas at Graceland

Christmas with Elvis at Graceland was always something special. For many years the tradition was to put all the decorations in place in early December, just after Thanksgiving, and keep them up through January 8, Elvis' birthday. A Christmas tree was placed in the dining room, often with another in the living room or other areas of the house. For the first Christmas or two at Graceland, Elvis decorated the front lawn with a large Santa, sleigh, and reindeers, with the message, "Merry Christmas to All, Elvis" suspended above it. In the sixties he switched to a life-sized Nativity scene, with lighted aluminum trees along the front of the house and blue lights outlining the winding driveway, a set-up he used each year from then on.

Elvis enjoyed Christmas, which was a special time for him and his family, friends, and staff. His generous nature was especially evident during the season of giving, with checks

Graceland with "Blue Christmas" lights along the driveway

Elvis' 1950s Santa and sleigh

and expensive gifts for the people in his life and annual donations to a long list of Memphis-area charities. Choosing a gift for Elvis, however, presented a challenge for those close to him, for here was a man who had everything money could buy. Gifts that related to his current hobbies or interests were always a good choice, but it was the gift that represented special thought on the part of the giver—not great expense —that meant the most to Elvis.

A sense of humor among Elvis' inner circle was ever present. Elvis, known for a radarlike sense of hearing, once overheard some of the guys in his entourage speculating about the size of their customary Christmas bonus, so Elvis decided to play a practical joke. On Christmas Eve that year, he handed out the traditional envelopes and watched their faces turn from smiling to horror stricken as they opened their $5 McDonald's gift certificates! When they figured out it was a joke, everyone broke into laughter, especially Elvis, who then handed out the real bonuses.

Today, the Graceland staff continues Elvis' Christmas decorating traditions. The decorations inside the mansion are authentic right down to the red holiday draperies used in the front rooms of the house during the late sixties and early seventies. The original Nativity scene and lights are set up on the front lawn, along with the old Santa and sleigh from the late fifties, which was found stored in the barn.

Since 1982, the Graceland staff has invited fans to send donations to the Memphis Chapter of the National Hemophilia Foundation, which sells poinsettias as an annual fund-raiser. These flowers are placed throughout the mansion for the holiday season. Visitors to Graceland can enjoy the holiday decorations from the day after Thanksgiving through January 8.

Over two million lights illuminate Dollywood for the holidays

A sign of the season, Pigeon Forge

Smoky Mountain Winterfest

Sevierville, Gatlinburg, Pigeon Forge, and Dollywood

A magical celebration of massive proportions begins with the flip of a switch on a mid-November evening in the Smoky Mountains. More than six million lights turn the towns of these parts into a winter wonderland of brilliant color and excitement. The lighting marks the beginning of literally dozens of holiday events in the sister towns of Sevierville, Pigeon Forge, and Gatlinburg, as well as in Dollywood, Dolly Parton's popular theme park.

Winterfest is the answer to what some of the country's most popular summer destinations do in winter. Started in 1990, the annual festival rapidly gained support from everyone who loves vacationing in the Smoky Mountains. The wealth of holiday entertainment includes arts and crafts shows, Christmas markets, plays, musical concerts and shows of all kinds, parades, festivals, dances, tours, open houses, road races, trolley rides, and—the most popular activity of all—shopping at thousands of craft booths, specialty shops, and the World's Largest Outlet Sale, which is held for ten days in mid-December.

In Sevierville the festival kicks off with the Five Oaks 5.5K race, which winds through the area's farms and apple orchards. The town continues its holiday celebrations with the annual "Parade of Toys," an open house in historic downtown, a children's hayride with Santa, a living nativity, and special performances in the Lee Greenwood Theater.

Visitors driving into Gatlinburg enter through a 200-foot tunnel of lights, which leads to a fantastic light show—a revolving 35 by 70-foot display that changes from a school house to Santa's workshop to a wedding chapel. The city's mascot, "Gatlinbear," waves greetings to passersby from several intersections. Gatlinburg's main light display is unique, for it is custom designed to detail the city's history and includes 40-foot-tall log cabins with smoke blowing out of their chimneys to commemorate the first homes here. There is also a three-dimensional bell tower, a 35-foot-tall fountain of light, and 20 beautiful chandelier archways draped across the street. And everywhere you'll see animated toys and Gatlinbears.

A winter street, Pigeon Forge

Three million of Winterfest's lights are found in Pigeon Forge, where they are fashioned into Mount Rushmore, the Golden Gate Bridge, the Liberty Bell, a crystal cathedral, and an 80-foot riverboat that seems to glide along the Pigeon River. While many visitors view the lighting displays from their automobiles, those who wish something a little more old-fashioned can see the lights on trolley tours.

Many well-known country music and comedy stars have theaters in the Pigeon Forge area. Most recently, singer Louise Mandrell opened the Winterfest season with her holiday show. The much-loved "Country Tonite" and long-running "Smoky Mountain Jubilee" join with the Memories Theater, the Dixie Stampede Dinner Show, and the Music Mansion Theater to offer their versions of the holiday spirit in music, drama, and dance. As popular as these activities are, none can outdo the wonderful shopping in Pigeon Forge's craft villages, specialty shops, and 200-store outlet center.

A native daughter of the Pigeon Forge area, Dolly Parton returned to her roots here by building Dollywood. Billed as Tennessee's number-one attraction, it is not just another amusement park, but an 118-acre theme park carefully designed to give visitors a sense of what life was like in Dolly's beloved Smoky Mountains when she was a young girl growing up. Dollywood preserves the regional traditions and crafts, and local craftspeople not only make and sell their goods here, but also teach others their skills and the history of their craft. Famous country and western stars perform at Dollywood, which also offers young musicians opportunities to perform—many up-and-coming artists received their first show business breaks here. Each December Dollywood hosts its annual "Holiday Deaf Awareness Day," when visitors with hearing impairments enjoy seasonal activities through interpretation, and children who visit Santa's Giant Workshop can tell Santa their Christmas wishes with the help of a "signing" elf.

Dollywood's Christmasfest celebration features two million lights and dozens of other attractions. It is a great place to shop for Christmas gifts, enjoy a variety of delicious holiday foods, and marvel at the beauty of the Great Smoky Mountains in wintertime. Carolers, gospel singers, and handbell choirs fill the air with the festive sounds of holiday music.

Peppermint Valley is a Christmas village filled with amusement rides. Kids of all ages enjoy Dollywood's antique Dentzel Carousel and taking a memory-making Yuletide journey aboard the 110-ton Fantasy Express steam train. Peppermint Valley is also the home of Santa's Giant Workshop, where Santa, Mrs. Claus, and a team of merry elves keep busy amid Christmas trees that actually talk and sing.

The mill in lights, Pigeon Forge

A magical place of lights and song and the spirit of Christmas, the Smoky Mountain Winterfest is the place you want to be come December in Tennessee.

 Christmas Eve there was always singing. Mama did most of it, but we all loved to sing along. She would always tell the Christmas story, and then Daddy would take us to the barn to see the animals kneel. The legend was that at the stroke of midnight, farm animals all over the world would kneel in honor of the newborn Jesus. Somehow we would always fall asleep before this happened. I suspect it was, at least in part, a way to get us to be still long enough to get sleepy, but it was a fine tradition anyway. Luckily there was something to get us to go to sleep. Otherwise, our excitement might have kept us up forever.

—FROM DOLLY BY DOLLY PARTON. *Copyright 1994, Dolly Parton.*
Used by arrangement with Harper Collins Publishers, Inc.

A Musical Tennessee Christmas

Nashville, Tennessee—one of the best-known music cities in the country—celebrates Christmas in song and symphony. For fifty-three years, the Nashville Symphony's annual Christmas concerts have captured the magic of the holiday season. Under the baton of Maestro Kenneth Schermerhorn and joined by a chorus of 150 singers, the seventy-five-member orchestra performs a number of concerts during the holidays.

The "Tennessee Christmas" concert, which annually headlines country star Amy Grant and many other country-western favorites, regularly plays to a sold-out audience of 12,000 at the Nashville Arena. This "very Tennessee" program has become so popular that the entire show now goes on the road, performing special engagements throughout Tennessee and neighboring states.

In early December, the symphony presents the beloved "Holiday Pops" concert, another sold-out performance held in the Tennessee Performing Arts Center. The special guests vary from year to year, but the concert is always a holiday favorite for all who attend.

The Nashville Symphony's performance of Handel's "Messiah," which features the Nashville Symphony Chorus, takes place in Ryman Auditorium, the original home of the Grand Old Opry. This 4,000-seat concert hall provides an intimate setting for this stirring Christmas classic.

The Nashville Symphony in concert

The Knoxville Choral Society performing Handel's
Messiah *at the historic Bijou Theater, Knoxville*

*I worked at the Bill Wilkerson
Speech and Hearing Center in
Nashville, where hearing, language
and speech disorders are diagnosed
and treated. Every November,
the Pi Beta Phi sorority alumnae
would organize a holiday craft
sale at the fairgrounds, with the
entrance fees benefiting the center.
The evening before the craft fair
opened, there was a special preview
show, worked by employees of the
center. My first year, I was a ticket
taker at the main door. The highlight of the evening was when
country star Amy Grant walked
through my door and said "Hi"
to me.*

—DR. WALT MURPHY,
formerly of Nashville

*The original estate of country music legend Conway Twitty, sparkling with
more than one million lights at Trinity Christmas City, Hendersonville*

Left and below: The Moscow State Ballet in the original Russian "Nutcracker," the Grand Ole Opry, Nashville

 We're a musical family and we love to sing carols while Michael, my husband, plays the piano. "Joy to the World" is the kids' favorite, but Michael likes "Angels We Have Heard on High" best.

—**MICHAEL AND RAMONA FREDMAN,** *Memphis*

The renowned Peabody marching ducks swim in the fountain of The Peabody Hotel, Memphis

The Dismembered Tennesseans playing old-time music for "An Appalachian Christmas," Chattanooga

TENNESSEE CHRISTMAS
by Amy Grant and Gary Chapman

Come on, weather man,
give us a forecast snowy white.
Can't you hear the prayers
of every childlike heart tonight?
Rockies are calling, Denver snow falling,
Somebody said it's four feet deep
But it doesn't matter, give me the laughter
I'm gonna choose to keep

Another tender Tennessee Christmas
The only Christmas for me
Where the love circles around us
Like the gifts around our tree.
Well, I know there's more snow up in Colorado
Than my roof will ever see
But a tender Tennessee Christmas
is the only Christmas for me.

Every now and then I get a wandering urge to see
Maybe California, maybe Tinsel Town's for me.
There's a parade there, we'd have it made there
Bring home a tan for New Year's Eve.
Sure sounds inviting, awfully exciting.
Still I think I'm gonna keep

Another tender Tennessee Christmas
The only Christmas for me
Where the love circles around us
Like the gifts around our tree.
Well, they say in L.A. it's a warm holiday
It's the only place to be.
But a tender Tennessee Christmas
is the only Christmas for me.

Old Farmer's Song of Winter

by Dick Poplin, Shelbyville

Sing a song of the winter time,
Far from the land of sunny clime,
Sing with the tune of the Christmas chime,
Supply the words and make them rhyme,
Fill your heart with cheer.

Sing of the ice, the snow, the sleet,
Of mittened hands and booted feet,
There's little to do but plenty to eat,
This is the season hard to beat,
The best time of the year.

Sing with the wind that whistles and moans
Around the eaves in somber tones,
The house contracts and cracks and groans,
Reminding us of the frigid zones.
The winter time is here.

Sing by the fire that crackles and pops,
While icicles form and mercury drops,
There'll be things to do when the snowing stops
But now relax and plan for the crops.
Of winter have no fear.

There're cows to milk and hogs to feed,
But no cotton to hoe nor corn to weed,
From summer's toil you now are freed,
So settle back by the fire and read,
Until the spring is near.

Reprinted with permission from A YARD OF POPLIN
by Dick Poplin, Bell Buckle Press, 1991.

Overleaf: Early morning snowstorm over Mount LeConte
Opposite: The Pugh Banjo, made from the bottom of a tin container, Museum of Appalachia, Norris

An Old English Christmas Fête

Where would you go to find a Christmas "fête" filled with English dancing, puppetry, Mummer plays, horn dances, plum pudding, boars head and wassail? Why Knoxville, Tennessee, of course.

Presented annually at the Laurel Theatre, this joyful event is eagerly attended by lords and ladies from town and country. They are heartily entertained by a lively company of crooners and dancers—groups with names such as the "Tenpenny Rapper Sword Dancers," "Sourwood Morris Dancers," and "Lark in the Morn Country Dancers." And a lark it is, with English recitations, dances and songs from the fifteenth, sixteenth, and seventeenth centuries.

Under the banner of the Jubilee Community Arts, the performers are joined by the well-fed and thoroughly amused assembly in topping off the evening with the singing of traditional Christmas carols. It may not be merry ol' England, but everyone agrees that a Christmas fête couldn't be better than the one held each year in Knoxville, Tennessee.

Top: Old English Christmas songs performed at the Laurel Theater, Knoxville

Left: Lark in the Morn English Country Dancers lining up for a stave dance, Knoxville

Spring house in the snow, Boone's Creek

Holiday Events

Blount County

Blount County Christmas Parade
First Saturday in December

Brentwood

Giving Peartrees
*Mid-November to
mid-December*

Tree Lighting
First Monday in December

Morning with Santa
First Saturday in December

Neighborhood Luminary Display
Second Saturday in December

Chattanooga

YMCA Christmas Market
First week in November

Regional History Museum's
Carriger Collection:
A Victorian Christmas
*Mid-November through
February*

Gifts Galore Holiday Market
Third weekend in November

Bluff View Art District
Holiday Open House
Friday before Thanksgiving

Grand Illumination and
Open House Downtown
Friday before Thanksgiving

Holiday Tour of Tables Festival
*Thanksgiving through
New Year's Day*

Rock City's Legends of Christmas
Daytime Program
*Thanksgiving through
New Year's*

Creative Discovery Museum's
Christmas Break
*Thanksgiving through
New Year's*

Bluff View Art District
Kicks Off Christmas
Late November

Rock City's Enchanted
Garden of Lights
*Late November through
early January*

Christmas Tours of Adams
Hilborne Mansion
Month of December

Love Lights a Tree Memorial Tree
Month of December

Christmas at the Courthouse
First two weeks in December

Victorian Holidays Open House
First Tuesday in December

Appalachian Christmas
First Friday in December

Singing Christmas Tree, the
Chattanooga Boys Choir
First Saturday in December

Annual Holiday Tea, Houston
Museum of Decorative Arts
First Sunday in December

The Nutcracker
Second weekend in December

Christmas on the River and
Holiday Nightlight Parade
Second Saturday in December

Christmas at the Hunter Museum
Second Saturday in December

Chickamauga Christmas
Train Tours
*Second and third weekends
in December*

Stories with Mrs. Claus
*Third Tuesday and Thursday
in December*

Chattanooga Girls' Choir
Winter Concert
Third Friday in December

Holiday Pops Concert
Third Saturday in December

Winter Carnival
Third weekend in December

New Year's Eve Block Party
New Year's Eve

Clarksville

Old Southern Christmas
Early December

Collierville

Christmas Tree Lighting
Ceremony
Early December

Christmas Parade
Early December

Dickens on the Square
Early December

Santa House
Mid-December

New Year's Eve Celebration
New Year's Eve

Columbia
(See Maury County)

Cookeville-Putnam County

Christmas Lights at Hidden
Hollow
*Thanksgiving through first
week in January*

Cookeville Christmas Parade
Monday after Thanksgiving

Monterey Christmas Parade
First Saturday in December

Breakfast with Santa
Second Saturday in December

Community Luminaria Lighting
Second Sunday in December

Covington

Christmas City
Month of December

Cowan
(See Franklin County)

Dayton

Christmas at the Courthouse
First Saturday in December

Franklin County

Annual Chamber Banquet,
Winchester
First Tuesday in December

Senior Citizens Craft Show,
Winchester
First Saturday in December

Annual Christmas Parade, Cowan
First Saturday in December

Candlelight Tour of Homes
First weekend December

Annual Dickens of Christmas
Mid-December

Christmas at Cedars of
Lebanon Park
Third week in December

Germantown

Germantown Holiday Parade
Mid-December

Santa's Talking Mailbox
Mid-December

Giles County

Milky Way Farm (Mars Family
Mansion) Open House
First Sunday in December

Public Library Trees of Christmas
First week in December

Highland Baptist Church
Living Nativity
Week before Christmas

Graceland

Christmas at Graceland
*Month of December
to January 8*

Harriman

Historic Cornstalk Heights
Christmas Home Tours
Second weekend in December

Hartsville-Trousdale County

Hartsville Hometown Christmas
First Saturday in December

Christmas Tour of Homes
Second Thursday in December

Hendersonville

Trinity Christmas City
(Conway Twitty Estate)
November and December

Christmas Heritage Home Tour
First Sunday in December

Christmas Parade
Second Sunday in December

Kingsport

Santa Train
*Friday and Saturday before
Thanksgiving*

Christmas Parade
Saturday before Thanksgiving

The Jesus Story, Appalachian
Fairgrounds, Gray
First two weekends in December

Christmas at Allandale Mansion
First weekend in December

Christmas in a Country Kitchen
First weekend in December

Yule Log Ceremony
First Sunday in December

First Night
New Year's Eve

Chipping of the Green
*First or second Saturday
in January*

Kingston
Annual Colonial Christmas Party
at Fort Southwest Point
First week in December

Kingston Christmas Home Tours
First weekend in December

Knoxville
Fantasy of Trees
Thanksgiving weekend

Christmas in the City
*Thanksgiving through
New Year's Eve*

Market Square/Krutch Park
Tree Lighting
First Friday in December

Santa Claus Parade
Second Friday in December

The Nutcracker
Mid-December

Nativity Pageant
Mid-December

Clayton Holiday Concert
Third week in December

Lynchberg
Christmas in the Hollow
First weekend December

Maury County
Plantation Christmas Tour
of Homes
First weekend in December

Christmas Parade
First Monday in December

McMinnville-Warren County
City Bank and Trust Craft Fair
Weekend before Thanksgiving

Christmas Parade
First Saturday in December

Memphis
Christmas Open House
Third week in November

A Holiday Walk in
Victorian Village
Third week in November

Peabody Annual Christmas
Tree Lighting Ceremony
Last week in November

Annual Christmas Exhibit
Last week in November

Playhouse on the Square
Christmas Play
Last week in November

Holiday Dazzle...Without a Frazzle
Last weekend in November

The Christmas Cottage
End of November

Annual Christmas Exhibit
December

Memphis Christmas Parade
December

Critter Christmas
Early December

Big One Christmas Show
Early December

Breakfast With Santa
Early December

Annual Peabody
New Year's Eve Party
New Year's Eve

Happy "Zoo" Year Party
New Year's Eve

New Year's Eve Festival
New Year's Eve

Moscow
Christmas Open House
December

Murfreesboro
Christmas Candlelight Tour
of Homes
Early December

Mount Pleasant
(See Maury County)

Nashville
A Country Christmas
November and December

Annual Nativity Exhibit
November and December

Christmas in the Park
November and December

Americana Christmas Sampler
Craft, Folk Art and Antique Show
Second week in November

Christmas Village
Mid-November

Trees Of Christmas
*Late November through
early January*

Festival of Lights
Weekends in December

Christmas Candlelight Tour
of Homes
Early December

Rudolph's Red Nose Run and
Christmas Parade
Early December

Christmas Open House:
Trousdale Place
First weekend in December

Plantation Christmas Tour
of Homes
Second week in December

Christmas at Two Rivers Mansion
Second week in December

Annual Dickens of a Christmas
Second week in December

Newport/Cocke County
Annual Christmas Gathering
Second week in November

Annual Christmas Parade
Last week in November

Christmas Bazaar
Last week in November

New Years Eve at Mimosa Manor
New Year's Eve

Obion County
Christmas Tree Lighting
First week in December

Pigeon Forge
Smoky Mountain Winterfest
Mid-November through February

Tellabration: A National Night
of Storytelling
Late November

World's Largest Outlet Sale
Mid-December for two weeks

Winterfest 5K Run
Mid-December

Winterfest Bridge Festival
Early January

Wilderness Wildlife Week of Nature
Two weeks in mid-January

Pulaski
(See Giles County)

Roane County
*(see Kingston, Harriman
& Rockwood)*

Rockwood
Rockwood Christmas Home Tours
First weekend in December

Sewanee
Annual Festival of Lessons
and Carols at The University
of the South
First Sunday in December

Shelbyville-Bedford County
Holiday Mixer
Thanksgiving weekend

Christmas in Bell Buckle
*First, second, and third weekends
in December*

Christmas Parade
Second weekend in December

Somerville-Fayette County
Annual Home for the Holidays
*Last week in November and first
week in December*

Walking Tour of Historic Homes
First Saturday in December

Sparta-White County
Christmas Fest
Second Tuesday in December

Sparta Rotary Club Christmas
Parade
Second Saturday in December

Chamber Christmas Window
Decorating Contest
Second week in December

Spring City
Rhea County's Annual
Christmas Parade
Second Saturday in December

Spring Hill
(See Maury County)

Springfield
Sugarplum Ball
Early December

Choral Society's "Messiah"
Mid-December

Townsend
Christmas at the Courthouse
First week in December

Townsend Christmas Parade
First Sunday in December

Williston
Christmas Tour of Homes
Throughout December

Winchester
(See Franklin County)

Thank You, Tennessee

Darlene Abbott
Lee Aguilera
Cindy Alford
Anne and William Allen
Bonnie Allin
Todd Andersen
Martha Andrews
Wallace Austin
Sheralee Michelle Azzone
Howard H. Baker, Jr.
Frances Baldwin
Diane Ballard
Mary Barnett
Gurnee Barrett III
Kreis and Sandy Beall
Adalene Weese
    and Richard Bell, Sr.
Tammy S. Berneking
Bluff View Art District
Lora Bolden
Shirley Boling
Gayle Bowling
Carolyn Brackett
Hank and Mary Brockman
Dan and Janet Brown
Sally Bush
Mary Cales
Terese Carbone
Brett Carter
Michael Chrisawn
Catherine Clark
Jennifer Cook
Al Corum
Laurel Crosby
Jim Davis
William B. Day, Jr.
Jed DeKalb
Bob Doll
Karen Dotson
Linda Eaves
Frank and Verne Ernst
Barbara Ethridge
Amon Carter Evans
Jan Fairchild
Fall Creek Falls
    three "volunteers"
Freddi Felt
Vilma Fields
Chef John Fleer
Eleanor W. Ford
Cynthia Ford-Sanders
R. C. Forrester

Fort Lauden State Park
Carlynne Foster
Judy Francesco
Joan Fredman
Michael and Ramona Fredman
Dr. and Mrs. William G. Fuqua
Marilyn Gargola
Chef Richard Gerst
Lisa Gordon
Kathie Gott
Chef Brad Grafton
Grand Ole Opry
Mary Belle Grande
Ralph Grindstaff
Karen Groom
C. Rita Groseclose
Carter and Joseph Hach
Phila Hach
Marilyn Harris
Janet Hasson
Bill Hawkins
Beth Henderson
Terry Hickey
Pat Hilton
Historic Rugby
Jane Ellen Hodges
John and Patty Holbrook
Jim Holmes
Loretta Hopper
Mary Hostettler
Hunt-Phelan House
Sonny Hunter
Catherine Hurst
Christy Ikner
Inn at Blackberry Farm
Anna Irwin
John Rice Irwin
Tim Jacobsen
Sally A. Jaunsen
Pam Jeffers
Judy Yost Jensen
Elizabeth Ann Johnson
Joseph E. Johnson
Ramona Jones
Hunter Kay
Christy Kemp
Darlene Kent-Abbott
Matt Kesterson
Nancy Waggener King
Diana Knoblach
Knoxville Choral Society
Amy Kottmeyer

Ken Kraay
Robert and Patricia Kraay
Salli LaGrone
Linda Tipton Lamb
Lark in the Morn English
Country Dancers
Betty Larkey
Susan Leach
Anne Locke
Carroll Logan
Ellen Long
Liz Lovell
Jane E. Lovett
Lisa Manning
M. Fred Marcum
Doug Marsh
Pat Martin
Mary Alice Mastellone
Billie May
Stephanie Maynard
Valerie McConnell
Craig McKinley
Tania Meek
Carolyn Meers
Michelle Merrifield
Elaine I. Meyer
Edna Miller
Yvonne Mingle
Jodee Mitchell
Peggy Montague
Moscow State Ballet
Marsha Mullin
Lois Brown Murphy
Walt Murphy
Museum of Appalachia
Betty Nagle
Angie Nichols
Helen Normand
Drew Ogle
Opryland Hotel
Frank Oros
Carla Parmele
Matt Peifer
LaDonna Pettis
Anna Platte
Dick Poplin
Noel Pourchot
Kay Powell
The Powell Family
Mrs. Jean Price
Anne Caldwell Ramsey
Rusty Reid

Martha Riddle
Walter Ring
Rick Roberts
Joe M. and Honey Rodgers
Johnna R. Rogers
Winifred C. Rose
Donald E. Russell
Jim Russell
St. Luke's Episcopal Church,
    Memphis
Beth Sams
Linda Sanders
Mary Ruth Schenck
Al Smith
Chef Kristie Smith
Todd Smith
Jane Springer
Barbara Stagg
Bette Stalnecker
Katherine Stephens
Sarah Moody Stinnett
Wilma Dykeman Stokley
Martha Sundquist
Judy Taylor
Phyllis and Roger Thomas
Aline Tipton
Jane Tolhurst
Kathy Torgerson
Charlotte Trentham
Alice Trimble
Kim Tuton
Linda Ullian
University of the South
Ralph Vaughn
Commissioner John Wade
Rev. Thomas R. Ward, Jr.
Judy Warren
Rebecca Miller Weeks
Gary White Deer
Debbie Whitworth
Tracey Elizabeth Williams
Ellen Williamson
Shelia Wilson
Linda Wise-Tucker
Sarah Yann
Linda Young
Carl Young
Shirley Yount

CHAMBERS OF COMMERCE

Anderson County
P.O. Box 147
Clinton, TN 37717
423-457-4542

Athens Area
13 N. Jackson Street
Athens, TN 37303
423-745-0334

Bledsoe County
P.O. Box 205
Pikeville, TN 37367
423-447-2791

Bolivar/Hardeman County
P.O. Box 313
Bolivar, TN 38008
901-658-6554

Brentwood
5211 Maryland Way, Ste. 1080
Brentwood, TN 37027
615-373-1595

Brownsville/Haywood County
121 W. Main Street
Brownsville, TN 38012
901-772-2193

Byrdstown/Pickett County
P.O. Box 447
Byrdstown, TN 38549
931-864-7195

Camden/Benton County
202 W. Main Street
Camden, TN 38320
901-584-8395

Campbell County
P.O. Box 305
Jacksboro, TN 37757
423-566-0329

Cannon County
Courthouse
Woodbury, TN 37190
615-563-2320

Chattanooga Area
2 Broad Street
Chattanooga, TN 37402
423-756-8687 or 800-322-3344

Cheatham County
P.O. Box 354
Ashland City, TN 37015
615-792-6722

Claiborne County
P.O. Box 332
Tazewell, TN 37879
423-626-4149

Clarksville/Montgomery County
180 Holiday Road
Clarksville, TN 37040
931-648-0001

Cleveland/Bradley County
2145 Keith Street
P.O. Box 2275
Cleveland, TN 37320
423-472-6587

Collierville Area
125 N. Rowlett
Collierville, TN 38017
901-853-1949

Cookeville/Putnam County
302 S. Jefferson Avenue
Cookeville, TN 38501
931-526-2211

Copper Basin Area
P.O. Box 948
Ducktown, TN 37326
423-496-9000

Covington/Tipton County
P.O. Box 683
Covington, TN 38019
901-476-9727

Greater Cumberland County
34 S. Main
Crossville, TN 38555
931-484-8444

Dale Hollow/Clay County
805 Brown Street
Celina, TN 38551
931-243-3338

Decatur County
201 Tennessee Avenue North
Parsons, TN 38363
901-847-4202

Dickson
119 Highway 70 East
Dickson, TN 37055
615-446-2349

Donelson/Hermitage
5653 Frist Boulevard, Ste. 740
Hermitage, TN 37076
615-883-7896

Dyersburg/Dyer County
P.O. Box 747
Dyersburg, TN 38025
901-285-3433

Elizabethton/Carter County
P.O. Box 190
Elizabethton, TN 37643
423-547-3850 or 800-347-0208

Erwin/Unicoi County
100 S. Main Avenue
P.O. Box 713
Erwin, TN 37650
423-743-3000

Etowah Area
P.O. Box 458
Etowah, TN 37331
423-263-2228

Fayette County
107 Court Square
P.O. Box 411
Sommerville, TN 38068
901-465-8690

Fayetteville/Lincoln County
P.O. Box 515
Fayetteville, TN 37334
615-433-1234

Franklin County
P.O. Box 280
Winchester, TN 37398
931-967-6788

Franklin/Williamson County
P.O. Box 156
Franklin, TN 37065
615-794-1225

Gainesboro/Jackson County
101 E. Hull Avenue
Gainesboro, TN 38562
931-268-0971

Gallatin
P.O. Box 26
Gallatin, TN 37066
615-452-4000

Gatlinburg
520 Parkway
P.O. Box 527
Gatlinburg, TN 37738
423-436-4178 or 800-822-1998

Gatlinburg Department of Tourism
234 Airport Road
P.O. Box 5
Gatlinburg, TN 37738
423-436-2392 or 800-267-7088

Gibson County
P.O. Box 464
Trenton, TN 38382
901-855-0973

Giles County
100 S. Second Street
Pulaski, TN 38478
931-363-3789

Goodlettsville
100 S. Main Street
Goodlettsville, TN 37072
615-859-7979

Greeneville/Greene County
115 Academy Street
Greeneville, TN 37743
423-638-4111

Grundy County
HCR 76
P.O. Box 578
Gruetli-Laager, TN 37339
931-779-3462

Hancock County
P.O. Box 347
Sneedville, TN 37869
423-733-4524

Hardin County
507 Main Street
Savannah, TN 38372
901-925-2364 or 800-552-FUNN

Hartsville/Trousdale County
200 E. Main Street, Suite 11
Hartsville, TN 37074
615-374-9243

Henderson/Chester County
P.O. Box 1976
Henderson, TN 38340
901-989-5222

Hickman County
P.O. Box 126
Centerville, TN 37033
931-729-5774

Hiwassee
P.O. Box 241
Ocoee, TN 37361
888-733-6263

Hohenwald
P.O. Box 819
Hohenwald, TN 38462
931-796-2731

Humboldt County
1200 Main Street
Humboldt, TN 38343
901-784-1842

Humphreys County
P.O. Box 733
Waverly, TN 37185
931-296-4865

Huntingdon/Carroll County
P.O. Box 726
Huntingdon, TN 38344
901-986-4664

Jackson/Madison County
Civic Center
400 S. Highland
Jackson, TN 38301
901-425-8333

Jamestown/Fentress County
P.O. Box 1294
Jamestown, TN 38556
615-879-9948

Jefferson City/County
532 Patriot Drive
Jefferson City, TN 37760
423-397-9642

Jellico
849 Fifth Street, Suite 1
Jellico, TN 37762
423-784-3275

Johnson City
P.O. Drawer 180
Johnson City, TN 37605
423-461-8000

Johnson County
P.O. Box 66
Mountain City, TN 37683
423-727-5800

Jonesborough
117 Boone Street
Jonesborough, TN 37659
423-753-1010

Kingsport
151 E. Main Street
P.O. Box 1403
Kingsport, TN 37662
423-392-8820 or 800-743-5282

Knoxville Area
810 Clinch Avenue
Knoxville, TN 37902
423-523-7263

Lauderdale County
110 S. Jefferson Street
Ripley, TN 38063
901-635-9541

Lawrence County
P.O. Box 86
Lawrenceburg, TN 38464
931-762-4911

Lebanon/Wilson County
149 Public Square
Lebanon, TN 37087
615-444-5503

Livingston/Overton County
P.O. Box 354
Livingston, TN 38570
931-823-6421

Loudon County
Dept. VG
P.O. Box 909
Loudon, TN 37774
423-458-2067

Lynchburg
P.O. Box 421
Lynchburg, TN 37352
931-759-4111

Macon County
208 Church Street
Lafayette, TN 37083
615-666-5885

Madisonville/Monroe County
P.O. Box 37
Madisonville, TN 37354
423-442-9147

Manchester
110 E. Main Street
Manchester, TN 37355
931-728-7635

Marion County
24 Courthouse Square
Jasper, TN 37347
423-942-5103

Marshall County
227 Second Avenue North
Lewisburg, TN 37091
931-359-3863

Maury County
P.O. Box 1076
Columbia, TN 38402
931-381-7176

McMinnville/Warren County
P.O. Box 574
McMinnville, TN 37110
931-473-6611

McNairy County
144 Cypress Avenue
P.O. Box 7
Selmer, TN 38375
901-645-6360

Memphis
47 Union Avenue
Memphis, TN 38103
901-543-5300 or 901-681-1111

Milan
1061 S. Main Street
Milan, TN 38358
901-686-7494

Millington
7743 Church Street
Millington, TN 38053
901-872-1486

Morristown Area
P.O. Box 9
Morristown, TN 37815
423-586-6382

Mount Juliet
P.O. Box 487
Mount Juliet, TN 37122
615-758-3478

Nashville
161 Fourth Avenue North
Nashville, TN 37219
615-259-4700

Newport/Cocke County
360 E. Main Street
Ste. 141
Newport, TN 37821
423-625-9675

Oak Ridge
302 S. Tulane Avenue
Oak Ridge, TN 37830
423-482-7821 or 800-887-3429

Obion County
P.O. Box 70
Union City, TN 38281
901-885-0211

Paris/Henry County
P.O. Box 8
Paris, TN 38242
901-642-3431

Pigeon Forge
2450 Parkway
P.O. Box 1390
Pigeon Forge, TN 37868
423-453-8574 or 800-251-9100

Polk County
P.O. Box 560
Benton, TN 37307
423-338-5040

Portland
P.O. Box 387
Portland, TN 37148
615-325-9032

City of Red Boiling Springs
P.O. Box 190
Red Boiling Springs, TN 37150
615-699-2011

Reelfoot Lake
Route 1
P.O. Box 1205
Tiptonville, TN 38079
901-253-8144

Rhea
107 Main Street
Dayton, TN 37321
423-775-0361

Roane County
P.O. Box 1033
Kingston, TN 37763
800-386-4686 or 423-376-4201

Robertson County
100 Fifth Avenue West
Springfield, TN 37172
615-384-3800

Rogersville/Hawkins County
301 E. Main Street
Rogersville, TN 37857
423-272-2186

Historic Rugby, Inc.
P.O. Box 8
Rugby, TN 37733
423-628-2441

Rutherford County
P.O. Box 864
Murfreesboro, TN 37133
615-893-6565

Scott County
P.O. Box 442
Oneida, TN 37841
423-569-6900 or 800-645-6905

Sequatchie County
P.O. Box 595
Dunlap, TN 37327
423-949-3479

Sevierville
866 Winfield Dunn Parkway
Sevierville, TN 37876
423-453-6411 or 800-255-6411

Shelbyville/Bedford County
100 Cannon Boulevard
Shelbyville, TN 37160
931-684-3482

Smith County
P.O. Box 70
Cathage, TN 37030
615-735-2093

Smithville/DeKalb County
P.O. Box 64
Smithville, TN 37166
615-597-4163

Smoky Mountain
201 S. Washington Street
Maryville, TN 37804
423-983-2241 or 800-525-6834

Smyrna
P.O. Box 864
Smyrna, TN 37133
615-893-6565

Sparta/White County
16 W. Bockman
Sparta, TN 38583
931-836-3552

Spring City
P.O. Box 355
Spring City, TN 37381
423-365-5210

Springfield
100 Fifth Avenue West
Springfield, TN 37172
615-384-3800

Stewart County
P.O. Box 147
Dover, TN 37058
931-232-8290

Sumner County
P.O. Box 957
Gallatin, TN 37066
615-230-8474

Townsend
7906 E. Lamar Alexander Pkwy.
Townsend, TN 37882
423-448-6134

Trenton
309 S. College
Trenton, TN 38330
901-855-2013

Tullahoma
P.O. Box 1205
Tullahoma, TN 37388
931-455-5497

Union County
P.O. Box 278
Maynardville, TN 37808
423-992-3061

Van Buren County
P.O. Box 814
Spencer, TN 38584
931-946-7033

Wartburg County
P.O. Box 387
Wartburg, TN 37887
423-346-6288

Waynesboro/Wayne County
P.O. Box 675
Waynesboro, TN 38485
931-722-9022

Weakley County
P.O. Box 67
Dresden, TN 38225
901-364-3787

STATE AND REGIONAL TOURISM OFFICES

Chattanooga Area
2 Broad Street
Chattanooga, TN 37402
432-756-8687

East Tennessee
531 Henley Street
Knoxville, TN 37902
423-594-5500

Greater Nashville
501 Union Street, 6th Floor
Nashville, TN 37219
615-862-8828

Main Street Collierville
P.O. Box 53
Collierville, TN 38027
901-854-6123

Middle East Tennessee
5616 Kingston Pike
Knoxville, TN 37919
423-584-8553

Middle Tennessee
320 Sixth Avenue North
5th Floor
Nashville, TN 37243
615-741-9045

Northeast Tennessee
P.O. Box 415
Jonesborough, TN 37659
423-913-5550 or 800-468-6882,
Ext. 25

Northwest Tennessee
P.O. Box 963
Martin, TN 38237
901-587-4215

South Central Tennessee
215 Frank Street
Lawrenceburg, TN 38464
931-762-6944

Tennessee's Back Roads Heritage Association
300 South Jackson
Tullahoma, TN 37388
800-799-6131

Tennessee Department of Tourist Development
320 Sixth Avenue North
Fifth Floor
Nashville, TN 37243
615-741-2159

Tennessee Natchez Trace Corridor Association
203 Third Avenue South
Franklin, TN 37064
615-794-5555

Tennessee Overhill Heritage Association
P.O. Box 193
Etowah, TN 37331
423-263-7232

Tennessee Tourism Information
P.O. Box 10
Parker's Crossroads, TN 38388
901-423-6937

Upper Cumberland Tourism Association
P.O. Box 2411
Cookeville, TN 38502
931-520-1088

West Tennessee
225 Martin Luther King
Suite 305
Jackson, TN 38301
901-426-0888

A TENNESSEE TASTE TEST

Just a week after Valentine's Day in 1998, in beautiful Central Presbyterian Church, Clayton, Missouri, a lively group of hungry folks gathered to taste the recipes submitted by Tennessee cooks. After several hours of feasting, the results were in—the favorite recipe was Christmas Stollen, followed closely by Egg Cheese Casserole, English Trifle, Streusel Coffee Cake, and Mushroom Casserole. We wish to extend special thanks to Amy Kottmeyer, who organized this successful affair and put so much hard work into making it so much fun, and to the many cooks and tasters who contributed their own special skills.

THE COOKS AND BAKERS

Gina Avery, Rebekah Blankenship, R. Josephine Carus, Kimberly Cook, June Fields, Julie Geisz, Barb Hartley, Paula Hays, Amy Kottmeyer, Laura Kurzu, Rosemarie Litteken, Jennifer Macalady, Joyce Merideth, Ida Pavioni, Tammy Rasche, Greg and Missy Reiter, Angela Ruggeri, Elizabeth Stephens, Kim Tuton, Nancy White, Bernie Williams, Ana Woodard.

THE TASTE TESTERS

Gina Avery, Julie Bergsma, Annie Blankenship, Bill Blankenship, Rebekah Blankenship, Rachel Busch, R. Josephine Carus, Kimberly and Robert Cook, Stacy Duckworth, June Fields, Andy Flach, Julie Geisz, Barb and Dave Hartley, Jeff and Lisa Hays, Ken and Paula Hays, Skip Jaeggi, Ariana and Tom Karst, Melissa Kiefer, Amy and Rich Kottmeyer, Laura Kurzu, Rosemarie Litteken, Jennifer Macalady, Joyce Merideth, Ida Pavioni, Steve and Tammy Rasche, Greg and Missy Reiter, Angela Ruggeri, Edie Scholten, Linna Stamper, Elizabeth and Tyler Stephens, Nancy White, Bernie Williams, Adam and Ana Woodard.

PHOTO CREDITS

Courtesy of Graceland, Division of Elvis Presley Enterprises, Inc. 108 (top, bottom), 109 (top, bottom)
Courtesy of The Hermitage   21
Courtesy of the Nashville Convention and Visitors Bureau   113
Courtesy of Phila Hach   94
Courtesy of the Pigeon Forge Department of Tourism 110 (bottom), 111, 112
Courtesy of Trinity Broadcasting Network   114 (bottom)
Crosby, David   front cover, 1, 2, 4-5, 9, 10-11, 12, 13 (top, bottom), 14 (top, bottom), 15 (top, bottom), 16, 17, 18 (top, bottom, 19 (top, center, bottom), 23, 24, 25, 26, 28, 30, 38, 39, 42, 47, 50 (top, bottom), 52, 53 (top, bottom), 54, 55 (top, bottom), 56, 57, 58 (top, center, bottom), 60, 61 (top, center, bottom), 62 (top), 63, 64-65, 68, 72, 75 (bottom), 76, 78, 80, 81 (top, bottom), 82, 83, 84-85, 86-87, 89, 90 (top, bottom), 91 (top, bottom), 92, 93 (center, bottom), 97, 98, 99 (top, bottom), 100, 114 (top), 115 (top left, top right, bottom left, bottom right), 116-117, 118, 120 (top, bottom), 121, 128
DeKalb, Jed   34 (top, bottom), 35 (top, bottom), 36
Dollywood Publicity   110 (top)
Gaylord Entertainment   66 (top, bottom), 67
Holmes, Jim   back dust jacket flap (bottom)
Hood, Robin (Courtesy of the Museum of Appalachia)   59
Irwin, Elizabeth   29
Kracht, Doug   back dust jacket flap (top)
LaFevor, Bill (Courtesy of Belle Meade Plantation)   33
Landrum, Greg   95
Lovett, Jane C.   7
Nagle, Betty   62 (bottom), 74, 75 (top), 88
Wright, David (Courtesy of Belle Meade Plantation) 32 (top, bottom)

We would like to extend our deep appreciation to the Inn at Blackberry Farm, Walland; The Opryland Hotel, Nashville; and Bluff View Art District, Chattanooga, for so graciously offering their facilities and the services of their staffs to assist in several of the food shots in this book.

For further information on use of stock photography from David Crosby's library, contact Westcliffe Publishers.

A. P. Stewart, Lt. General, CSA, shares the Christmas spirit, Chattanooga